Assyrians in Western Media

The New York Times: 1851 – 1922

Edited by Ninos Warda

Published in the United States 2010 by the Assyrian Academic Society
Email: info@aas.net
Website: http://www.aas.net

ISBN: 978-0-9827124-3-6

Introduction

This book is a collection of important and rare articles from the world-renowned newspaper, The New York Times, reproduced for the first time as a book. The articles selected for this book range from the period 1851 to 1922, a time of intrigue, upheaval and uncertainty for the Assyrian people. This period, spanning close to a century of Assyrian history, marks one of the most critical and paradoxically one of the least studied areas in modern Assyrian history, covering a number of landmarks: the first western contact with the Assyrians; the trials and tribulations of World War I; forced migration from ancient lands; and the search for a future homeland. All of these issues are aptly covered in this timely book.

The articles, which are not exhaustive, have been found in the online archives of The New York Times and have been chosen with the specific aim to shed light on and provide a rare insight into the social, religious, cultural, and political life of the Assyrian communities in both the homeland and the ever-growing Diaspora.

As an example, it is hoped that the articles can help clarify the often-confusing and contentious name issue that has surrounded the Assyrians for decades. As a direct result of this confusion, the reader will find that the articles refer to the Assyrians using a number of different appellations, such as Chaldeo-Assyrian, Syrian, East Syrian, Nestorian, Jacobite, Chaldean, etc., all of which refer to the same people, thus further fueling the confusion. As one writer noted in an article written in 1918, found on page 74 of the book, referring to the Assyrians as 'Syrians' unnecessarily confuses them with the inhabitants of Syria. In the words of the contributor, "Failure to keep clear the distinction between Assyrians and Syrians has often led to great confusion."

Another way in which it is hoped these articles can help shed light on the identity issue is to counter a claim made by some scholars and historians that the English priest, Rev. William Ainger Wigram, was responsible for giving the name 'Assyrian' to the members of the Church of the East, then more commonly known as Nestorians, and propagating it. As the reader will find on page 1 of the articles, in 1879 an article was published under the title 'Churches and Ministers', where reference was made to the Assyrians under 'Home and Foreign Events'. The reference reads as such:

> "The Society for the Propagation of the Gospel in Foreign Parts is about to establish a mission at Mosul, in behalf of the Assyrian Christians."

The importance of this reference lies in the fact that it was written when Rev. Wigram, born in 1872, was only seven years old, thus rendering the claim by some that he was responsible for terming the Nestorians 'Assyrians' as historically inaccurate.

The articles have been helpfully organized in chronological order, allowing readers to pinpoint with ease any specific date or timeframe, and are of importance because they provide not only a contemporary viewpoint of various Assyrian issues but also contain eye-witness testimonies and accounts, many of which may have been lost had they not been recorded in these articles.

The articles have been selected in such a way so as to cover a broad spectrum of issues, and they have been included either because the article makes a direct reference to the Assyrians or concerns an issue directly or indirectly impacting upon them, such as for example articles reporting news on the secret Sykes-Picot Agreement between the British and the French, or the British expeditions in Mesopotamia.

The text of the articles has been reproduced exactly as was found in the original versions, even if original spelling mistakes with regards to proper nouns were made, and next to each article headline will be found the date on which the article was published in The New York Times. Any other mistakes found throughout the articles are solely of the editor.

Finally, special thanks go to Mr. Romeo Hanna of Sydney, Australia, whose help in collecting material for this book was indispensable. It is hoped that this publication will become an essential research tool and will attract the attention of scholars, historians, and readers in general.

Ninos Warda
Executive Director
Assyrian Academic Society

Assyrians in Western Media

The New York Times:
1851 – 1922

Missionary Intelligence – November 4, 1851

The monthly meeting of the Missionary Committee of the American Board was held yesterday. The attendance was large, and the proceedings were more than usually interesting.

Nestorians. – A letter from Mr. Cochran, dated August 16, gives a general account of the preaching department of the Nestorian Mission. In the city of Oroominahiort Seir, Geag Tapa, Ardeshai, Degala and Ada, there are at least two regular services on the Sabbath. At Charbosh, Vazerona, and five other villages on the plain of Barandoorz, and at three on the river between the city and Seir, there has not been less than one service every Sabbath; and at five or six other villages meetings have been frequent. The preaching department is still altogether inadequate to the wants of the people.

Churches and Ministers – December 28, 1879

Home and Foreign Events.

The Society for the Propagation of the Gospel in Foreign Parts is about to establish a mission at Mosul, in behalf of the Assyrian Christians.

The Test of Baby Clothes – October 24, 1880

It was the custom among the Nestorian Christians, immediately upon the conclusion of the marriage ceremony, to carry the newly made wife to the house of her husband's parents, and place an infant in her arms and three sets of baby clothes before her. If she succeeded in dressing and undressing baby three times to the satisfaction of the critical matrons there assembled, well and good; but if she failed she was sent to her old home again, to stay there, a wife and no wife, until able to face and pass a second trial. – *Chamber's Journal.*

A Chaldean Priest's Loss – March 3, 1884

Father Denha Epiphanius Barjona, a venerable Catholic priest from a little village in Chaldea, complained bitterly yesterday at the Capucin Convent of St. Fidelis, in Thirty-first-street, where he is now staying, that he had lost all the certificates and papers which proved his identity. He had been paying a visit to St. Francis Xavier's Church and had dropped the documents in Sixteenth-street. Father Barjona, who is a feeble old man with flowing white beard and hair, is an enthusiast on religious matters. A few months ago he started from his little Chaldean village and came to this country for the purpose of making collections for a church which he desires to build in his native village. He has been traveling all through the country, having brought from Rome, where he has numerous friends, letters of introduction to the Bishops of Cincinnati, St. Louis, Baltimore, and other dioceses. The old gentleman only speaks Chaldaic and Latin. His success through the country has not been very great, though he has received several contributions to his fund. He is to travel through France and Switzerland in pursuance of his object, and will leave here on Wednesday for the former country, the French Consul of this city having given him a free pass.

A Massacre of Christians – April 14, 1889

Terrible Atrocities in Kurdistan – The Porte Responsible.

To the Editor of the New-York Times:

In some of the London and New-York journals of last Autumn there appeared a telegram from Teheran, Persia, which stated that a rising of the Kurds against the Christians in the Julamerk division of the province of Van (in Turkey) had been reported by some English missionaries; that inquiry had been made of the Vali of Van and the reply received that the report was groundless. So the matter seems to have ended, so far at least as the public journals are concerned. Having in my possession, as a member of a committee which for several years has been assisting these Assyrian Christians, numerous letters from various officials of the Assyrian mission, perhaps you will allow me to state what really did occur in order that your readers may judge how far the report was "groundless."

The mountains of Kurdistan, close to the Persian frontier, are the home of the Chaldean or Assyrian Christian tribes. The largest of these tribes is the Tiari, inhabiting a valley of the lesser Zab, south of Julamerk.

3

It is the custom of these tribes to send their sheep in the summer to a zoma, or mountain pasture, in charge of their women. Last Summer the sheep of Ashitha, the largest village of Tiari, were being fed in a zoma near some Kurdish tribes which had always been considered friendly toward the Christians, in charge of about 300 women and girls and two men. On July 31 the encampment was suddenly surrounded by a large body of Kurds, and the two men being first murdered, all the women and girls were violated, five were killed under circumstances of terrible atrocity, several other wounded by dagger thrusts, and the rest stripped entirely naked and left in that state to make their way back to Ashitha. The consequences of this fearful outrage were not unnatural; the men of Tiari, wild with grief and indignation, seized their flint-lock muskets, and in spite of the entreaties of their chiefs and their clergy, prepared to meet the Kurds, who are mostly armed with Martini rifles, to avenge the honor of their wives and daughters. Against them there then assembled the Kurdish tribes Goagali, Zereknalu, Berwarnaii, and Sindaii, the authors of the outrage, together with other tribes in overwhelming numbers, computed at 15,000 fighting men, though probably not much exceeding 10,000. At this juncture the Rev. W. H. Browne, priest of the Archbishop of Canterbury's Assyrian mission, who happened to be in the district, sent a special messenger across the Persian frontier to Canon McLean, the head of the mission at Urmi. The Canon instantly telegraphed to the nearest British authorities in Persia, and the Turkish authorities in the province of Van, hearing of this action, and alarmed at the publicity given to the affair, at last took steps to prevent the impending massacre, at the same time assuring the British representatives that the report of any disturbance was "groundless." Thus an indiscriminate slaughter of Christians has been prevented, but the honor of the unfortunate women cannot be restored to them, nor those cruelly murdered brought to life again.

It is not to obtain redress for the past, but in the hope of arousing public opinion and of making such outrages less possible in the future that this letter is written. The province of Van, including Hakkiari, where these Christians live, is inhabited by three races, the Armenian, the Kurd, and the Assyrian. The "Armenian Question," or the enforcement of Article 61 of the treaty of Berlin (local reforms in favor of the Armenians and their security against Kurds and Circassians) is, of course, a burning one in this province, and the present object of the Porte appears to be to play off the Kurds

4

against the Armenians by raising a "Kurdish question," in opposition to the "Armenian question," in other words, to bring to the front these wild and lawless Mohammedan tribes as a difficulty in the way of granting favors to their Christian Armenian fellow-subjects. The Assyrian, East Syrian, Chaldean, or Nestorian Christians (for by all these different names they are known) constitute a third factor, and so stand in the way of this policy; it has been the fashion in times past to ignore them; now the Turkish authorities appear to have resolved upon their utter destruction. Their condition is an absolutely helpless one; they are the only Christians who have no representative at Constantinople, and are thus entirely at the mercy of the local Governors. Though numbering nearly 100,000 souls in Turkey, they have literally no one among them of sufficient education to represent them officially, and but very few that can speak Turkish, the official language. Their Patriarch, Mar Shimun, and his Council are ignorant of the rudiments of Turkish law, and know neither how to formulate their grievances nor how to seek redress.

Only a short time ago, when they were daily expecting the onslaught of the Kurds, the only thing the distracted, helpless creatures could suggest was that telegrams for protection should be sent to the Queen of England, the Archbishop of Canterbury, and the King of France! Poor people, they are a little behind the times in their knowledge of politics and history. The Porte has hitherto successfully prevented any schools being established among them by either native or foreign agencies on Turkish soil, though on the Persian side of the frontier, thanks to a decent Government, no hindrances are offered to education. They are of no political value, they are not intriguers, but simple shepherds, and it has never occurred to anybody to insert a clause for their benefit in any treaty. If your readers wish to form an idea of the sufferings of the population, whether Christian or Mussulman, in the Turkish provinces the consular reports of Great Britain will show the heartless oppression and the utter corruption of the officials. It would be amusing if not too sad to trace in each case the result of English influence. The Consul selects the worst cases and reports them to her Britannic Majesty's Embassy at Constantinople. Her Britannic Majesty's Embassy complains to the Turkish Minister of the Interior, and the Minister replies that he will make inquiries. Some months afterwards he sends a polite message to her Britannic Majesty's Embassy that, having made a strict investigation, he finds the consular report "greatly exaggerated" or "groundless," and so the matter drops. Such is the state of affairs in those parts of the empire which, through the Consuls, are more or less under the eye of Europe. What happens in more remote districts the tragedy of last July sufficiently exhibits.

It appears to be the object of the Porte to sweep away altogether the Assyrian Christians. Whole villages, the property of their Christian inhabitants from time immemorial, have been sold to the Kurdish chiefs, their hereditary enemies, be it remembered. In these cases there are only two courses open to the unfortunate villagers, starvation or beggary in Russia. I ought perhaps, in justice, to state that since the arrival of the Archbishop of Canterbury's clergy, (four Oxford and Cambridge graduates sent out at the request of Mar Shimun,) the same year this particular form of outrage has been suspended, owing, probably, to the residence of Europeans in the country. The Porte has, however, made the most strenuous efforts to rid itself of the presence of these clergymen by harassing them in every possible way. Canon Maclean, after travelling through Hakkiari, was put under arrest for eight days at Jezireh in September, 1887, and Mr. Browne was arrested at Diza, on the Persian frontier, and detained for five days the following November.

In November of last year the Porte, believing that the story of last Summer's awful tragedy had been forgotten, demanded of the English Government the withdrawal of the Rev. Mr. Browne. Angered because that faithful priest informed the British authorities in Persia of the murders committed and of the impending massacre, the Porte has determined that this obstacle in the way of the wholesale destruction of the Assyrian Christians shall be removed and the path made easier for future massacres. What the British Government in its anxiety to preserve peaceful relations with the Porte, and thus check Russia's advance upon the East, may do in this matter is not easy to determine. But is it not time for Christians of every land, America as well as Europe, to call for a cessation of these infamous outrages that are blackening one of the fairest portions of God's heritage?

J. CHAUNCEY LINSLEY
GENERAL THEOLOGICAL
SEMINARY. NEW-YORK,
Saturday, March 13, 1889.

Assyrian Christians – September 22, 1889

The Ashiret Assyrians are wild and untutored in their habits and customs. Their Christianity consists in little more than a passionate clinging to a faith they do not comprehend, and which from this very fact is powerless to influence their morals. Not only are there no schools among them, but their clergy are incapable of instructing their flocks in the rudiments of religion; some of them are quite unable to conduct a service, others can repeat the important parts by heart, while a few can read the ancient manuscripts, which are still in daily use throughout the country because there are no printed books. It is comparatively rare to find a priest who can both read and write with facility; all other learning is absolutely wanting. Only during the Winter months, when the snow blocks the entrances to the mountains, when all agriculture is at a standstill and Kurdish attacks become impossible, could these Ashirets give their minds to education; in the past Winter the Rev. W. H. Browne of the Archbishop of Canterbury's mission, has been able to make a very small beginning in this direction. During the rest of the year the people till their ground, and pasture their flocks armed to the teeth, ready to repel the attacks of which they live in constant dread. Indeed, the Ashiret Assyrians are in the position of a beleaguered garrison in a siege which is never raised; an unending succession of assaults and sorties leaves them neither time nor inclination to think of more peaceful matters. Their whole conversation is limited o three subjects – guns, the Kurds, and the harvest. On one occasion during my journey through the Ashiret valleys in 1886, after vainly trying to interest a chief in conversation, it occurred to me that a description of the Maxim gun might arouse him. The man's face brightened at the relation of the marvelous powers of the weapon, and when I had finished he said: "Ah, if we only had a gun like that we should not fear the Kurds! No man could make such a gun; it must have been invented by the angels!" – *The Contemporary Review.*

Assyrians Bound for Chicago – May 3, 1893

One Thinks Elevated Trains Fast and Avenue Coaches Like Camels.

It looked as if an Oriental garden had found a place in the Holland House yesterday when down the main stairway walked an Assyrian dressed in bright golden and purple robes. He paused at the foot of the stairs, where some palms are growing, and, with the background of the plants and the banks of roses beside them, gave the ladies who were coming out of the dining room a picture that was both rich and unusual.

The Assyrian wore a flowing gown of red, with yellow bands across it and flowing trousers of yellow silk reaching to his knees. Numerous bands of silk were wound around his body and his neck. His legs below the knee were covered with dark, reddish-brown bands. A fez cap was on his head.

He passed out of the hotel. Presently there began to come other Assyrians. They wore the clothes of the ordinary immigrant. The only badge which stamped them as from the Orient was the fez which each wore.

They were a party bound for the World's Fair, and the reason for their call at the Holland House was that Mr. Sursock, the Commissioner from Asiatic Turkey, who had them in charge, was stopping there.

Some of them spoke broken English. They said they had studied the language for two years in Assyria.

"What do you think of New York?" a NEW YORK TIMES reporter asked one of them.

"Great, very great," he said.

"Have you had a ride in the elevated cars?"

"Yes; fast, very fast," was the reply.

"Have you been in one of the coaches up Fifth Avenue?"

"Yes, shake very much, like camels."

Most of the party started for Chicago last night.

Assyrians Wedded in Trinity – May 8, 1893

Took an Hour and a Half to Make Miss Mary Abo Reehan Mrs. N. Abo Samra.

Trinity Church had its first Assyrian wedding yesterday. The contracting parties were N. Abo Samra, an Assyrian merchant, of 74 West Street, and Mary Abo Reehan.

The bride, who is only seventeen years old, was attired in the conventional white dress and orange blossoms, and the groom wore a black frock coat and gray trousers. The Rev. Christopherus Jeberah, Archimandrite in the Greek Church, who has been in this country only a few weeks, tied the knot, and it took him an hour and a half to do it. Trinity Church was thronged with the friends of the bride and groom, and with many who were attracted by the novelty of the ceremonies.

The Rev. Mr. Jeberah wore all his robes of office. Over a black gown he put on a long chasuble of white silk, embroidered with gold, and on his head he wore a high golden hat, which looked like a helmet of the time of the Crusaders.

The bride was attended by a single bridesmaid, and there were no ushers. A choir of boys chanted responses to the priest's intoning, standing with long wax candles in their hands, on the right side of the altar.

In the course of the ceremony, both bride and groom were crowned with flowers, and when the final words had been chanted, these were removed and thrown aside. The friends of the happy pair, who sat in the pews of the church, held lighted candles in their hands during the service. When it was ended, the candles were extinguished and carried away as mementos.

The service was conducted entirely in the Greek language. At its close, the newly-wedded pair entered a carriage and were driven away without the usual accompaniment of rice and old slippers.

Syriac Wedding Service – October 29, 1894

A Quaint Oriental Celebration in Washington Street.

A beautiful Impromptu Poem Precedes the Marriage – A White Rosary Placed on the Groom's Head and a Black One on the Bride's Head – Fares A. Ferzan Takes Miss Sassol Maloof for His Bride – A Picturesque Assemblage at the Ceremony.

These existing features move me more than eloquence;
So here stand I, joy be the consequence.
This hall is gay with limpid lustre bright;
These seated guests pick at the spiced food,
And drink profusely, for the cheer is good.
This royal wedding is world renowned.

This original poem, given just as it was written, was the closing feature of the ceremonies which last night made Fares A. Ferzan and Miss Sassol Maloof man and wife.

The poem was read by its author, Mr. Amin Rihan, a young man who has stage aspirations, but who for the present is engaged in trade, like most of his fellow Assyrians in New-York.

In an introductory speech, he said:

"I know not how I shall offend in expressing these unpolished words to you, nor how the world would censure me for choosing so strong a prop, (gracefully waving his hand toward the bride and groom,) to support so unworthy and weak a burden."

He stood on the steps of the altar, which the priest had just left, and faced the bridal couple. He had followed Elias Ferzan, the groom's brother; N. A. Mankarzel, a friend of the groom, and another young man, all of whom had read original poems in Arabic. He was applauded by the picturesque Assyrian friends of the bride and groom, and the knowing nods of his own intimate friends showed how much his genius was appreciated.

The ceremony was performed by Mgr. Karkamez, in the Maronite Church of St. Peter's. The church is on the top floor of 81 Washington Street, which from the outside has all the appearance of an old warehouse. After climbing up three narrow flights of stairs the guests found themselves in a large room, whose board walls had been covered with a brown-figured paper and the ceiling with white paper. A long black stovepipe extends half the length of the ceiling, and ended abruptly in the middle of the room, at the place where a stove probably is placed in cold weather.

At one end of the room was a small altar, on which stood lighted candles and the various sacred ornaments seen in the Catholic Church.

The bride, a rosy-cheeked, black-eyed Assyrian, dressed in white figured silk, trimmed with lace, and wearing the customary tulle veil and orange blossoms, stood between the groom, in evening dress, and her bridesmaid, Mrs. Hafiza Ayob, who was dressed in cream-colored chiffon, trimmed with lace, and wore on her head a dotted tulle veil. Both ladies wore white kid gloves, and the bride had diamonds in her ears, and on her breast a dainty gold watch rested, studded with diamonds.

On the left of the groom stood his best man, Salim Elias, in a black suit, sack coat, and white silk four-in-hand tie. Back of the bridal party were crowded the wedding guests, each holding a lighted candle. They were mostly Assyrians, but dressed in all kinds of costumes. A few wore the flowing Oriental garb. Pretty girls were bareheaded, veiled, or bonneted as suited their whims. One man had a bandage on his head and wore his soiled working clothes. Two or three boys wore "sweaters," one had on his

messenger's uniform, and two or three men wore evening dress.

After the priest had blessed in Syriac the two rings to the chanting, always in Syriac, of a young man, he placed them on the little fingers of the bride and groom. A white rosary was blessed and placed on the groom's head, where it dangled in his eyes and swept his nose. He showed no annoyance, however.

A black rosary was placed on the bride's head, a white rosary on the best man's wrist, and a black one on the bridesmaid's wrist.

The usual questions were asked the bride and groom, and their hands were joined together by the priest, who covered them with his stole.

Then came the congratulatory poems, and the crowd hurried down stairs. It was no easy matter to get the bride's huge trunk down stairs and onto the hack which was to carry the pair to the railroad station. Their trip is to include Canada, Niagara Falls, Boston, Providence and finally Atlantic City, where the groom lives. He is the proprietor of a bazaar in that city. The bride's father is Nazem Maloof, a silk merchant, of No. 73 Washington street.

Kurds and Christians – January 16, 1895

Some of the Oppressions and Cruelties in Times of Peace.

Christians were Bought and Sold

In Some Districts They Were Forced to Work Without Recompense – Constant Raids on Villages.

In this week's number of The Independent will appear an article on "The Kurds and Christians Before the Massacres," showing to what kind of life these Armenian, Jacobite, and Nestorian Christians are condemned in times of peace.

These facts, from trustworthy sources, are given in this article:

As showing the exactions made on the common people by the Government, it is stated that Mustapha Pasha, a nomad chief, in 1893 collected 4,000 piasters (4.4 cents each) from the village of Mansurieh of Bohtan, and claimed 5,000 more, although the villagers acknowledge owing only 2,000 piasters. Fourteen persons in this village were assessed a double tax for several years, amounting to 4,000 piasters. Bashibazouks took 2,000 piasters' worth of barley and other produce from the village without payment.

Mustapha Pasha bought the tithes of the villagers from the Government for 7,500 piasters and collected 9,000. When the villagers complained to the Government they were not redressed, but Mustapha Pasha sent flocks of sheep which devoured 2,000 piasters' worth of growing crops.

The legitimate taxes for the village for 1893 were 14,000 piasters, but, in addition, 12,500 piasters were collected. Mansurieh is only one hour from Jezireh, the Government headquarters. Nothing was done to protect it.

Hassana of Bohtan is a village of 60 houses. The Aghas of Shernakh exacted from the villagers of Hassana 1,160 piasters in 1891, 1,739 piasters in 1892, and 8,074 piasters in 1893, as noted at the time of the occurrences by a village priest. The total for the three years, 1891-3, was 10,873 piasters, as against 5,376 for the three years 1880-82, showing that the exactions are increasing.

A Christian of the District of Berwer has put in writing what he has seen of the oppression of Christians by Kurds. He saw numerous murders-and mentions the names of eight victims - three robberies of considerable amounts, and many smaller ones.

Mohammed Bey of Berwer is responsible for these and other crimes. In the same district the Kurds made the Christians build their castles, sow and harvest their fields, and do much other labor, without recompense. Not only this, but cursings and beatings were showered on Christians as they worked. Sundays were special days of oppression.

Besides all this, the Kurds of other districts raided the villages of Berwer, killed the inhabitants like dogs, burned their houses, and carried away their goods. Duree, My, Eyrt, Ina, and D'Noony suffered in the greatest degree.

The village of Mar Yokhanan has been raided several times during the last two years. So has Maragha, only a short distance away. A number of Christian villages further back in the mountains were even more severely oppressed. The people were bought and sold as slaves. In other districts the buying and selling of Christians by Kurds is common.

The people of Shakh were forced to live in caves in the mountains in Winter, because of extortionate taxes which necessitated their giving up their homes. The priest's house was forcibly entered, his life threatened, and his goods carried away.

Nahrwan, near Jezireh, is on the plain within easy reach of the Government. It is visited daily by the Kurds from the mountains, who exact the usual tribute of produce and money. This last Summer the demands were so excessive that, rendered desperate, the villagers seized one of the Kurds who stopped over night in a neighboring village, recovered some of their goods, and took possession of his guns. They did this without violence to him.

A few days after, this Kurd, with his followers, waylaid two of the men of this village, one of whom escaped. The other was carried some miles to a river, where he was stabbed to death and his body flung into the river. The murderers were well known, but nothing was done toward apprehending them.

The writer was in Nahrwan when the Kaimakam of Jezireh came, several weeks after the affair, to examine into it. The examination was rendered so oppressive to the Christians that the people were glad to declare that nothing had happened, in order to escape any further inquisition. Even the old mother of the murdered man was frightened until she declared that she did not know of any such occurrence, and had no complaints to make against anybody.

Other villages which were raided and the cattle stolen, the inhabitants murdered, or forced to flee to the mountains, or at least to send their women and children away, are Kannybalaver, Dihi of Supna, Bebabi, Dari, Kumani, and Mosul.

Four years ago a Christian priest of Dari, who had secured an education and acquired some influence was appointed by the Nestorian Patriarch, agent for the Christians of that district. In his efforts to secure redress for his people and to protect them from the exactions of the Kurds, he incurred the hostility of those who had been living off their villages. One evening, on his way to Dari, only half an hour from the city, he was shot down by these Kurds.

There were two companions with him who saw the Kurds who did the killing and recognized them as well-known men. They were so intimidated, however, by the Kurds that they have never dared to make accusation or give testimony against them. Nothing was done by the Government.

Last Spring two Christians who had sold their sheep in Mosul and were on their way home were attacked by Kurds just outside of the city. They left their animals and fled. The Kurds pursued them, overtook one of them, and shot him down. The sum of money taken was considerable. The wounded man was brought to the house of one of the missionaries, where he lay for several months before he recovered sufficiently to return to his home.

Through the influence of the missionaries the Government was induced to take action; two men were arrested against whom there seemed to be strong evidence. The case was allowed to drag along from month to month, until finally the prisoners were released, and nothing further was done.

The district of Zabur, adjoining the District of Amadia, not many years ago was well populated with Christians, there being a number of Christian villages. To-day there is not a single Christian village, they all have been taken by the Kurds. The few families left live in practical slavery to the Kurds.

An old missionary, who has been familiar with the region from Bohtan to Amadia, for years, says these oppressions are increasing, and unless something is done speedily all the Christian villages of these various districts will soon fall into the hands of the Kurds, just as they have in Zabur.

The villages of Mansurieh, Shakh, and Hassana have been given as examples of such oppression; but as the evil is general, affecting all Christians in Turkey, it is proper to summarize these abuses as generally practiced. The legitimate taxes are exceedingly heavy, but additional burdens are laid upon the people through the following abuses, which are merely mentioned and classified.

Abuses through unjust and corrupt assessment.

Villages are compelled to give Assessors presents of money to prevent them from overestimating the taxable persons and property in the village.

Assessors, to secure additional bribes, signify their willingness, for a consideration, to make an underestimate. The ignorant villagers gladly avail themselves of the opportunity, in order to recover what they have given the assessors in presents and bribes. This, however, affords an opportunity for blackmail, which is used by succeeding officials. It also afterward involves them in trouble with the Government, in which they suffer loss.

Injustice and severity in collecting.

The collectors, as a rule, go to the villages on Sunday, as on that day they find the people in the village. They frequently interrupt the Christian services and show disrespect to their churches or places of prayer.

The collection of the taxes is accompanied with unnecessary abuse and reviling, sometimes even with wanton destruction of property.

Even after several failures of crops in succession, when famine was so severe that the people were many of them being fed by foreign charity, the taxes were collected in full and with severity.

Their food supply, beds, household utensils, and farming implements were seized by the Collectors in lieu of taxes. Many were compelled to borrow money at enormous rates of interest, mortgaging their fields and future crops. Unscrupulous officials and other Kurds, in whose interests such opportunities are created, thus became possessed of Christian villages, the people of which henceforth becoming practically slaves to them.

These collectors make false returns of taxes received. The official in the city is secured by a bribe, and the matter is kept quiet until a succeeding set of officials comes into office. They send their officers to the villages to present claims for back taxes. The villagers in vain contend that they have paid them. They have no receipts. They do not dare to ask for them. Or the head man of the village who keeps the accounts has been bribed to falsify his accounts. These taxes are collected again, entailing much suffering upon the people.

The books in the Government offices at the Kaimakamlik are often incorrect through mistakes or dishonesty, and in consequence taxes are paid on fictitious names or on persons who have been dead for years.

Taxes are often farmed out to the highest bidder, who usually is some powerful Kurdish chief. Either in consequence of his power, or by means of bribes, he is secure from interference on the part of the Government. He collects the amount due the Government and then takes for himself as much as he chooses, his own will or an exhausted thrashing floor being the only limit to his rapacity.

While he is collector for these villages they are considered as belonging to him.

All the assessors and collectors - and they are many, a different one for each kind of tax, personal, house and land, sheep, tobacco, &c. - on their visits to the villages, take with them a retinue of servants and soldiers, who, with their horses, must be kept at the expense of the village, thus entailing a very heavy additional burden upon them. Soldiers and servants sent to the villagers to make collections very naturally take something for themselves.

The Government has recently established a system of loans on mortgages to the farmers, ostensibly for their relief, but undoubtedly for the purpose of securing their land, as the farmers will never be able to pay even the interest on the loans.

The Yezidis are a remnant of a heathen sect, who have never been converted to the Moslem faith.

Their holy place is not far from the City of Mosul, one day's journey, and their principal villages are also close by. In the Summer of 1892 the Sultan sent a special officer, called Farik Pasha, to Mosul to correct certain abuses in the Government, to collect all back taxes, and to convert the Yezidis. His authority was absolute, the Vali Pasha of the city being subject to his orders.

In reference to his work among the Yezidis, he, it was generally reported, was to get a certain sum per capita for every convert made.

He first sent priests among them to convert them to the "true faith." They not succeeding, he very soon gave them the old alternative of the Koran or the sword. Still not submitting, he sent his soldiers, under command of his son, who put to the sword all who, not able to escape, refused to accept Mohammed. Their villages were burned, many were killed in cold blood, some were tortured, women and young girls were outraged or carried off to harems, and other atrocities, too horrible to relate, were perpetrated.

Those who escaped made their way to the mountains of Sinjar, where, together with their brethren of the mountains, they in-trenched themselves and successfully defended themselves until the Spring of 1893 against the Government troops which had been sent against them.

This massacre was reported to the French Government by M. Siouffl, Consul at that time in Mosul, and to the English Government by Mr. Parry, who was in that region under the instructions of the Archbishop of Canterbury.

The Yezidis who remained in their villages on the plain had Moslem priests set over them to instruct them in the Moslem faith. They were compelled to attend prayers and nominally become Mohammedans; but in secret they practiced their own rites and declared that they were still Yezidis.

No Persecutions in Persia – March 11, 1896

Armenians and Other Christians Well Treated by the Shah.

Tehran Dispatch in London News.

At a time when the treatment of Christians in Turkey forms a subject of European concern, it will perhaps be of some interest to inquire into the condition of Christians in a neighboring country.

Persia, like Turkey, is an Islam country, and nearly the whole of her inhabitants are Mohammedans – the non-Mohammedans forming hardly one-twentieth of her entire population. The tenets of the Sheah sect, followed by the State and eleven-fourteenths of the whole population, are perhaps more exclusive and less tolerant than those of Sunni professed by Turks. The Christians, composed of Armenians and Chaldeo-Syrians, number altogether about 130,000. They chiefly inhabit the provinces of Aragh and Azerbaijan, though a few of them are also found in other parts of the country.

The Armenians in Aragh number a little less than 40,000; they are found in Teheran, Julfa, (near Ispahan,) and Resht, but mostly in villages east and northeast of Ispahan. In this part of the country they are neighbors of the Loris, one of the wildest and most lawless tribes in all Persia. In Azerbaijan the Armenians number over 40,000. They are found in the principal towns and in the districts of Urumia and Suldouz, but chiefly in those of Salmas and Karadagh. The Chaldeo-Syrians, who number a little less than 50,000, inhabit mostly villages in the districts of Salmas, Urumia, Sinneh, and Sakkiz. The bulk of the people belong to the Nestorian sect, although many of them have of late years embraced Catholicism or Protestantism. The Christians in Azerbaijan are generally neighbors of or intermingled with Persian-Turks and Kurds, the later being as wild as the Loris. Readers of the foregoing statements might be led to consider that Persia in these conditions is the worst place for Christians to live in. But facts prove the contrary.

Kajar Kings in general, and the present sovereign in particular, have never made any difference between their Moslem and non-Moslem subjects – Christians, Zoroastrians, Jews, and other non-Mohammedans and semi-Mohammedans. All have, in comparison to other Asiatic countries, enjoyed liberty in religious matters. In matters of education the Government have in no way tried to meddle with them

or to interpose the least obstacles, nay, the Shah has always been very favorably disposed to educational institutions. He has granted, besides occasional presents, perpetual pensions to chief Christian and non-Mohammedan schools.

Justice in Persia is administered according to the Sheri and to the Orfi. The Orfi is the law formed by customs and precedents. The Sheri is the law formulated and compiled in conformity with the precepts of the Koran and its commentators. The Christians are free to go to one or to the other. They have also the right to appeal to the mediation of their spiritual chiefs, and, in very many cases, to be judged by them.

When, some time ago, news of troubles in Turkey began to reach Persia, first as rumors, then to be confirmed and detailed by hundreds of letters written by Persian merchants in Anatolia to their correspondents in this country, the Government, justly apprehending lest the contagion of pillage and robbery might be caught by the wandering tribes and the lower class in the country, sent, and continued to repeat, most stringent orders to provincial and district Governors to take strict measures to keep order, and to redouble their vigilance that the tranquillity of Christians in no case might be disturbed; moreover, rendering all in authority responsible for any disorder which might happen within their jurisdiction. This timely precaution saved many a trouble to the Christians in Azerbaijan, and their tranquillity was not disturbed through the events in Turkey.

Now, how is it that the Persian Government, with innumerable drawbacks, have been able to insure the tranquillity of their alien subjects and of the country at large, while the Turkish Government with many advantages at their disposal, with laws and administration framed more or less after European ideas and system, and with strong civil and military organizations, have failed to content their non-Ottoman subjects? This question must be answered by the friends of Turkey, and by those who are versed in the affairs of that country.

Conversion by Wholesale – September 6, 1897

Constantinople Telegram in The London Chronicle.

Among the Nestorian Christians inhabiting the frontier lands of Persia and Turkey came a number of Russian missionary priests last May, representing that the Archbishop of Canterbury's protection was useless and that they had better join the Russian Orthodox Church, thus securing moral and material protection. In consequence, the whole Church, numbering 300,000 in Persia and 100,000 in Turkey, including many Protestant converts, have joined the Russian Orthodox Church.

War on Christians in Persia – January 25, 1898

A Student in Illinois Learns that His Cousin was Tortured to Death.

CARLINVILLE, Ill., Jan. 24.- The Mohammedan priests in a large village near Ooroomiah, Persia, have declared a jahad, or holy war, against the Nestorian Christians. This is the home of Joseph Badel, a missionary student of Blackburn University, in this city. He has received authentic information that his cousin, an influential man, was tortured to death in the bazaar and his home burned.

Many Christians have fled, leaving their possessions behind, while forty have placed themselves under the protection of the Russian Consulate at Labriz. The soldiers sent by the Governor General for protection commit even more outrageous atrocities than the populace.

Christians Killed in Persia – July 21, 1900

Persian Student In Peoria Informed that a General Massacre Is Imminent.

CHICAGO, July 20.- A dispatch from Peoria, Ill., says George Shimoon, a Persian student, who has been attending college in Illinois for several years and is passing the Summer in Peoria, to-day received a cablegram from his home, at Oroomiah, Persia, stating that his brother had been murdered by Mohammedans and that a general massacre of the 3,000 Christians in Oroomiah was expected.

The cablegram states that the feeling of the Mohammedans against the native Christians is growing and that there have been several hand-to-hand battles, with fatalities on both sides. Mr. Shimoon's father is a native missionary, and this fact adds to the wrath against him and his family.

Turks Massacre Persians – August 6, 1907

6,000 Troops Cross the Frontier and Destroy a Village.

TEHERAN, Aug. 5-Incursions of Turkish troops across the northwest frontier of Persia have again begun.

A serious raid has occurred near Urumiah, 6,000 Turkish troops, with artillery, having crossed the frontier and destroyed the village of Mavaneh. Seventy-eight villagers, of whom sixty were women and children, mostly Christians, were killed. Subsequently the Turks drove a small force of Persian troops from a near-by camp and installed themselves in it.

According to an unofficial report a large body of Persian cavalry subsequently joined the Turkish invaders, and the combined force is said to be threatening the town of Urumiah, twelve miles west of Lake Urumiah and sixty-four miles from Tabriz.

Urumiah, which has a population estimated at between 30,000 and 50,000, including many Christians, is noted as a centre of missionary activity, and is the seat of the Fiske Seminary for Girls and of Urumiah College.

It is considered probable that Russia and Great Britain will be appealed to and will bring pressure to bear upon Turkey with a view to stopping the raid.

Persia Appeals to Russia – August 8, 1907

Says the Invading Turkish Troops Are Burning and Slaying.

ST. PETERSBURG, Aug. 7.- Persia has asked the assistance of the Russian Foreign Office in obtaining a settlement of her frontier dispute with Turkey. She asserts that Turkish troops have penetrated a distance of forty miles into Persian territory, terrorizing the population by fire and sword.

The original delimitation of the Turko-Persian frontier was made by Russian and English surveyors in the sixties.

TEHERAN, Aug. 7.- The latest advices from the border say that the Turkish troops which recently crossed the north-west frontier of Persia are marching on Urumiah, burning and devastating villages along their route.

The Christian village of Mewan is reported to have been shelled and ninety persons, including many women and children, are said to have been killed. Ten girls were carried off.

A panic prevails at Urumiah.

Prince Firman Firma, the Minister of Justice, has been appointed Governor of the province of Azerbaijan, the scene of the trouble, and has been ordered to take up his duties immediately.

The government is consulting with the foreign representatives regarding the Turkish invasion.

To Stop Raid in Persia – August 12, 1907

Ports Issues Orders to Troops - A Patriotic Persian Governor.

CONSTANTINOPLE, Aug. 11.- Thanks to the influence of the British and Russian ambassadors and the representations of the Persian Ambassador here, there seems to be a prospect of a satisfactory settlement of the Turco-Persian incident.

The Porte has instructed the Turkish commander at Bagdad to stop all forward movement of troops and has dispatched Frontier Commissioners to the scene to make inquiry as to the responsibility for the incident.

TEHERAN, Aug. 11.- Prince Firman Firma, the newly appointed Governor of the Province of Azerbaijan, is displaying great activity and patriotism in connection with the Turco-Persian frontier incident. He appeared before Parliament yesterday and announced that he had arranged for 10,000 men to be in readiness to proceed to the frontier, and that he would bear the entire cost.

Parliament offered the Prince £75,000 toward the cost of the expedition, but he declined to accept it.

Kurds Persecute Persians – August 26, 1907

Trouble Over the Turks' Raid Threatens to Become Serious.

CONSTANTINOPLE, Aug. 25.- The Government is dispatching a special commission of officials of high rank to the Turco-Persian frontier to open an inquiry regarding the recent invasion by Turks of Persian territory and the blood-shed and destruction of property that followed. The Porte repudiates the allegation that Ottoman troops advanced beyond the frontier.

Reports received here say that the matter threatens to assume a grave character, especially as the Persian inhabitants of the district are being severely persecuted by Turkey's Kurdish auxiliaries.

Turks Take Persian Town – October 6, 1907

British Consul Sets off to Protest to Turkish Governor.

TABRIZ, Persia. Oct. 5- Turkish troops yesterday occupied the town of Askerabad, Persia, thirteen miles from Uramia. There is an unconfirmed report current here that the town of Salmas also was taken by the Turks. The British Consul at Uramia has left there for Marwana to make representations in the matter to the Governor of Bitlis.

The incursions of Turkish troops across the Persian Frontier, of which the occupation of Askerabad is an example, began last summer. After Persia had protested, the Porte sent a commission to investigate the occurrences. The reason of the invasion is to be found in the rival claims to a contested territory. The situation is inflamed by religious hatred.

Nestorian Tablet Moved – November 15, 1907

Placed in a Siang-fu Temple, Out of Reach of the Vandals.

PEKING, Nov. 14.– The Governor of Shen-Si has removed the Nestorian Tablet from its ancient exposed situation in an open field outside the capital, Siang-fu, and placed it in the Peilin Temple, inside the walls of the city.

It is assumed that the increasing number of European vandals in the province since 1902 aroused the Governor's fear that the tablet would be stolen.

The Nestorian Tablet, which was erected in 781 A.D., records the arrival at Siang-fu, then the capital of the Chinese Empire in A. D. 635 of the Nestorian priest Clopun from Syria, and gives a brief summary of the Nestorian Christians in China from A. D. 635 up to 781. The Nestorians were a sect of Christians named after Nestorius, a Patriarch of Constantinople, who lived in the fifth century.

Kurds Raid Armenia – December 27, 1907

Town of Urumiah Completely Isolated – Many Caravans Pillaged.

ST. PETERSBURG, Dec. 26.- A dispatch from Urumiah, in Persian Armenia, which was bought out by a detachment of Russian troops, states that for the last eight days that town has been entirely surrounded and isolated by bands of Kurdish raiders, who have attacked caravans and driven hundreds of loaded camels to the mountains.

A caravan escorted by the guards of the Russian Consulate at Urumiah, which was the first to get through, was attacked by fifty bandits. The robbers were repulsed, many of them being killed or wounded. Complete anarchy prevails at Urumiah.

Russia is planning to strengthen the Consulate guard there, but it is declared in St. Petersburg that the time for actual intervention has not yet come.

Miss Gould Entertains – March 22, 1908

Students from the Orient Her Guests at Tea.

Miss Helen Gould gave a reception and tea to a number of Oriental students now studying in New York, at her home, 570 Fifth Avenue, yesterday afternoon. There were students, women as well as men, from Japan, India, Assyria, and other Oriental countries, as well as many young Americans, who are studying in New York.

After the reception, at which Miss Gould introduced her sister, Mme. Anna Gould, to the students, the guests provided an entertainment.

The Misses Datterson, Debow, and Bain, the American girl students at the Institute of Musical Art, sang the oratorio from Elijah; a Japanese girl talked about Japan; a Hindu girl told of India, and an Assyrian girl lectured on her ancient fatherland.

6,000 Miles to See His Son – September 12, 1910

Aged Assyrian Arrives Safely, Though He Had Little to Guide Him.

Special to The New York Times.

PASSAIC, N. J., Sept. 11.- With only an address on a slip of paper to guide him Alahmed K. Himadi traveled alone 6,000 miles from Assyria to this country to visit his son, Dr. David A. Himadi of Lodl.

So overcome with joy was the elder Himadi when he saw his son that he fainted. They had not seen each other for fifteen years.

Discoveries at Nineveh – September 20, 1910

Death of Hormuzd Rassam Recalls His Famous Suit Against Budge.

To the Editor of The New York Times:

The recent death of Hormuzd Rassam recalls some interesting circumstances.

In 1893 Mr. Rassam (in Queen's Bench, Rassam vs. Budge) sued Dr. Budge, the Curator of the Department of Oriental Antiquities in the British Museum, for slander and libel, in saying and writing that he, (Rassam,) while in charge of the excavations at Abbo-Habba, had permitted his relatives to carry away and dispose of the best finds for their own advantage and had only sent "rubbish" to the British Museum, which employed him. These charges Dr. Budge had made to Sir Henry Layard, M. Renouf, and Dr. Pinches, all of whom testified at the trial that Budge had made them. They had also been made in writing to the Trustees of the museum.

Before bringing suit Mr. Rassam showed the Trustees that he had had no relatives at Aboo-Habba, or within several hundred miles of it; that he had not permitted any antiquities to be carried away, and that he had not sent "rubbish" to the museum.

Whereupon Dr. Budge wrote him what he (Budge) considered and asserted was a retraction and "full apology," but which the court characterized as "insincere, ungentlemanly, and shabby." Upon receiving this unsatisfactory retraction Mr. Rassam took his grievance to the High Court of Justice, where he was overwhelmingly supported by the evidence, firmly upheld by Mr. Justice Cave, and, contrary to every expectation, denied justice by the jury, who rendered a verdict for defendant.

Mr. Rassam was a very sensitive man, then nearly 70 years of age, and this miscarriage of justice nearly broke his heart. Despairing, on account of his foreign birth, (he was a Chaldean,) of ever obtaining justice from a British jury, he confided his papers to me and begged that when he had passed away beyond the sphere of calumny and injustice I would relate his story to the world. He was a sincere Christian, honest, frank, and communicative, but of a shy, timid, and retiring disposition, ready to yield to almost any domination.

His story commences in 1845, when he conducted those excavations at Nineveh which have rendered the name of Layard famous; for it was Rassam and not Layard who made the discoveries, Rassam who could read cuneiform, Rassam who could converse with the natives in Chaldee or Arabic, and not Layard, who understood only English and French, neither of which was of the slightest use in Mesopotamia, and who therefore could do nothing but look on while Rassam worked. The latter declared one day to me in the British Museum that the name of Layard on the great human-headed bulls and on other Assyrian monuments should in truth be erased and his own substituted, "for it was I," said he, "who sought for these antiquities, I who found them, and I who sent them to the museum, not Layard." He also told me of the bargeload of cuneiform tablets which Layard sank, or permitted to be sunk, in the Tigris, leaving me to guess at the reason for it. When I hazarded a conjecture he would neither confirm nor contradict it. "Sir Henry," said he, "has always been kind to me, and I can say nothing to his disadvantage." This was just about the time when he was bringing suit against Dr. Budge. His story of what was done, and what was not done but should have been done, at Nineveh, Kouyunjik, and Aboo-Habba, would fill a volume, but a volume that I fear will never be written, for nobody would believe it, and what's the use?

ALEXANDER DEL MAR.
New York, Sept. 18, 1910.

Report Christians in Peril in Turkey – November 12, 1914

Views of Refugees Now in Petrograd – All Men Forced Into the Army.

Special Cable to THE NEW YORK TIMES.

PETROGRAD, NOV. 11, (Dispatch to The London Morning Post.) - Refugees who have arrived here from Constantinople report that the state of things there and in Turkey generally is appalling.

Brigandage, murder, and atrocities are committed. Armenians being the chief victims, but all Christians and foreigners are in great danger.

One refugee, a Greek, tells me he ran away to escape forced military service, leaving his wife and his mother behind. According to his account the Turkish authorities are forcing every man possible into the ranks of the army.

The fighting on Saturday and Sunday at Koprikos was not renewed on Monday, but the day was spent in a vigorous artillery duel, apparently without result. In the meantime Russian columns are marching up in two directions to reinforce each other for an attack on Erzerum.

Several strategic points of the utmost importance are already in the hands of the Russians.

Turkish People's Misery – December 5, 1914

Missionaries Tell of Terrible Conditions – Raids by Kurds.

The American Board of Commissioners for Foreign Missions has issued a bulletin relative to conditions in Turkey which contains excerpts from letters recently received in this country from missionaries in Turkey. Some of them read:

A. N. Andru of Mardin. - Everything is in confusion, trade is utterly paralyzed, travel is impossible, transportation is stopped, schools are stripped of their teachers, money has ceased to circulate, drafts cannot be cashed, grain remains unthrashed and unwinnowed for lack of animals and men to do the work; the labor market is closed, and hunger in the midst of plenty is already looking in at the door of thousands of whence two, three, four, and, in some cases, five of the breadwinners have been summoned to the ranks.

E. C. Woodley of Marash. - Churches cannot pay pastors' salaries and we cannot help because of our shortage of funds. From one of our best outstation churches seventy-two out of ninety-four male members have been called out as soldiers.

E. C. Partridge of Sivas. - Everything that is movable is being taken from shops and in some cases from houses. Thousands of villagers have been sleeping hungry in the streets of Sivas for three weeks, while their wheat is wasting in the fields.

Mary D. Uline of Bitlis. - If ever relief was needed it is now. People will starve to death and die of exposure. Hundreds and hundreds of wild Arabs and Kurds from the south have been going through the city on their horses. They helped themselves to whatever they wanted from merchants and travelers.

Mutiny in India Urged by Germans – March 19, 1915

British Government Says Pamphlets Were Addressed to the Troops.

LONDON, March 18.- The India Office announces that Documents have reached the British Government showing that German Consular officials in Persia and agents of German firms have been engaged in intrigues, with the object of facilitating a Turkish invasion of Persia and promoting an uprising of the tribes against Great Britain.

The German Consul at Bushire, on the Persian Gulf, who is now stationed at Shiraz, aided by Germans and Indians from Berlin, has, says the India Office, been circulating pamphlets addressed to the Indian Army calling upon the soldiers to "throw off the hated yoke and rise and kill your officers."

A long appeal to the Mussulman soldiers was also found, urging them to join in a "jehad" (holy war).

Telegrams are made public by the India Office, which, it says, show that arms and ammunition consigned to the German Legation at Teheran were received through Bushire. These supplies were to be used to arm the tribesmen, who were to attack Bushirc.

The Foreign Office was advised today that Turkish soldiers recently ran wild in the Urumiah district of northwestern Persia and killed several hundred civilians. The Turks are said to have burned several villages after looting them.

Turkish Consul Led Mob to Our Mission – March 22, 1915

Russians Report Attack on Priests – Send Troops to Save Christians.

PETROGRAD, March. 21.-A dispatch from Julfa, Persia, to the Westnik News Bureau, the official Russian news agency, says:

"The Turkish Consul at Urumiah, Mehemed Raghib Bey, at the head of seventy Askari, recently attacked the American mission at that place, where 15,000 orthodox Christians had taken refuge. The Consul ordered three priests and two deacons to leave the mission, and as they were passing through the streets they were insulted and mercilessly beaten.

In the courtyard of the orthodox mission a gibbet was erected.

An American missionary, Mr. Allen, who was also subjected to insults and blows, succeeded in sending to Selmas two messengers to ask for prompt assistance from the Russian troops to save the lives of the Christians, whom the mission was not able to protect."

Hang a Bishop in Our Mission – March 26, 1915

Turkish Regular Troops at Urumiah Also Kill Four Orthodox Priests.

A MISSIONARY IS BEATEN

Mr. Allen Insulted – Dr. Packard Risks Life by Showing Flag and Averting Massacre.

WOMEN TAKEN AS SLAVES

Men Murdered by Turks and Kurds – Christians Held Out Till Their Ammunition Was Gone.

TIFLIS, Wednesday, March 24, (via Petrograd and London, March 25.)- Telegrams and letters reaching here from Urumiah, Northwestern Persia, describe the situation of the American Presbyterian Mission stationed there as desperate. Turkish regular troops and Kurds are persecuting and massacring Christians.

Dr. Harry P. Packard, the doctor of the missionary station at Urumiah of the Board of Foreign Missions of the Presbyterian Church, risked his life in a successful effort to prevent a frightful massacre at Geogtopa, where 3,000 Persian Christians made their last stand. They had fought for three days, and all their ammunition was gone. At this juncture Dr. Packard unfurled an American flag and advanced between the lines. His act resulted in the saving of all but 200 of the Persian Christians, who had been burned in a church.

Fifteen thousand Christians have taken refuge under the protection of the American Mission station, while 2,000 are at the French Mission.

A dispatch received at Tiflis from Urumiah yesterday said that seventy Turkish regular troops had entered the mission, hanged the Orthodox Bishop, Mar Elia, and four Orthodox clergymen, and beaten and insulted a missionary named Allen. Shortly before that sixty refugees had been dragged from the French Mission and executed in spite of the pleas of the nuns.

Slain in Groups of Five.

At Culpashan the Kurds were particularly cruel. This was the last of a total of 103 villages to hold out, and it was occupied a month ago. The Kurds ordered all the male citizens into the streets, tied them in groups of five, marched them to the graveyard, and killed them barbarously to the last boy. Girl babies and the older women were then executed with great atrocity, while the younger women were carried away as slaves.

As a result of the war 12,000 Persian Christians are taking refuge in the Caucasus, some 17,000 are described as in imminent danger at the Urumiah Missions, while 20,000 are dead or missing. Furthermore, much property has been destroyed.

The Christians fought their assailants bravely, and as long as they had ammunition they were victorious.

The missionaries are untiring in their efforts to help the people, and they are spending money to this end freely. In Urumiah they are disbursing the equivalent of $400 daily.

Disease is prevalent among the refugees.

Nothing Heard from Morgenthau.

WASHINGTON, March 25.- Continued reports of menace to the lives of American missionaries and refugees at Urumiah, Northern Persia, have aroused the activity of the State Department. Although only one official communication on the subject has been received, Secretary Bryan stated today that diplomatic and consular officials in Persia, Turkey and Russia had been apprised of the reported circumstances and appealed to for any available information.

Nothing was heard by the department today on the subject from Ambassador Morgenthau, at

Constantinople, who yesterday was directed by the department to urge the Turkish Government to afford protection to Americans at Urumiah.

NORTH YAKIMA, Wash., March 25.-The missionary named Allen mentioned in today's telegram from Tiflis is the Rev. Dr. E. T. Allen, a brother of Mrs. E. V. Lunn of North Yakima. He was at one time pastor of a church in Portland, Ore.

Dr. Allen is a naturalized American. His wife and three children are with him at Urumiah. The latest letter Mrs. Lunn received from her brother, dated December, says in part;

"The very people that we visited some months ago to help are now howling outside the city gates, waiting to shed our blood, if they can force their way in. There are thousands, and we do not have much food."

Mission Board Gets News.

At the offices of the Presbyterian Board of Foreign Missions, 156 Fifth Avenue, it was learned yesterday that a cable had been received on Wednesday from a native Christian of the mission at Urumiah, confirming in detail press dispatches from Tiflis, but omitting mention of the part which Dr. Packard played in safeguarding the Americans under his charge. Special mention was made in the cablegram of the destruction of the French mission at Gulpashan.

The American missionaries at present in Urumiah are the Rev. F. G. Coan and Mrs. Coan, the Rev. W. A. Shedd and Mrs. Shedd, the Rev. C. C. Sterrett and Mrs. Sterrett, Miss Mary E. Lewis, Miss. E. D. Lamme, Harry P. Packard, Mrs. H. P. Packard, Mrs. J. P. Cochran, the Rev. Hugo A Mueller and Mrs. Mueller, the Rev. E. T. Allen, and Miss Lenore R. Schoebel.

Dr. Packard has been in charge of the Mission for some years, having returned to Urumiah from a vacation in the United States a few months ago. At that time it was suggested that he be transferred to another, more important mission, and a petition signed by the most powerful of the Mullahs (Mohammedan Priests) and the Sayids (Moslem nobles) was presented to the board, begging that Dr. Packard be retained. The friendship of these dignitaries was due in large part to the fact that many of them had been patients in the hospital which is a part of the mission at Urumiah.

Until the telegram arrived on Wednesday no fear had been entertained in this country as to the safety of the missionaries, as it was known that the native tribes were particularly friendly to the American mission and the foreigners attached to it. Another cause for hopefulness was the fact that in October, when the situation became critical, the Russian Consul begged Dr. Packard to remain, as he thought that the moral effect of his presence might accomplish more in the way of quieting the natives than his guard of 800 Cossacks.

"Historic Nation Annihilated."

The people of Urumiah, who are members of the Assyrian Christian Church, are described as "a historic nation with noble traditions annihilated" in a letter just received by THE NEW YORK TIMES from an American minister who fled to Tiflis when the Russian Army left Urumiah and the Kurds swept down upon the district. The letter, which is dated Tiflis, Feb. 10, says in part:

"From what we can gather the villages of Urumiah plain, those inhabited by Christians, some seventy in number, have been nearly all of them plundered, some burned to ashes, many young men killed, young women taken captive by Kurds and Persian Moslems, churches desecrated and demolished. Some 15,000 Assyrian and Armenian Christians from Urumiah have fled to Russia.

"The province of Aderbaijan, in Northwestern Persia, was occupied by the Russian Army, and for the past two or three years the Moslems and Christians alike enjoyed peace and prosperity, the roads for commerce were open, and there was personal security for all natives and foreigners alike.

"Some two months ago it was feared that for strategic reasons the Russian Army in Urumiah might be withdrawn for other centres. Still, an effort for the sake of the Christians was made, and the Russians stayed and repulsed the Kurdish attack on every side. The Kurds were mainly and solely coming for plunder and revenge. In this the low classes of Persian Moslems became partners.

"The Russian Army was suddenly recalled from Urumiah, Solmas, Tabriz and elsewhere. The Baranduz and Uri River people knew nothing of this withdrawal from Urumiah, as the Russian Army was to pass westward. The eastern section of the villages knew nothing of the evacuation till the Russians had left and the roads were blocked.

"The Baranduz men, true to their traditions of bravery, kept defending the villages and women after the Russians had left. They were armed already by the Russians and were doing well in keeping villages from daily attacks. The women and children of the villages had been sent to Geogtopa, the largest Christian village, five miles east of the city, and after the young men could not keep the Kurds back, they fell on

Geogtopa, where they fought the hordes of Kurds for two days. The Persian Moslems, from the city, came from the rear and assisted the Kurds.

"The scene that followed was horrible. The young men were killed, the young women taken by the Kurds and Moslems for themselves. The village was burned and plundered, together with all the churches. The two rich villages of Culpashan and Charojushi have not been burned, one Kurdish chief having appropriated them for himself.

"We have telegraphed to the President of the United States for relief of those in Urumiah. It is to America that we look for assistance and guidance. Let our young men there know their duties to what may be surviving of their families. Money can be sent to Persia through the American Consul at Tabriz and the American Consul at Tiflis. The money should be sent, through the representatives of the districts in which men live, to the State Department. We invite the Red Cross people to come to our assistance in our deep agony."

Turks Continue Urumiah Slaying – March 27, 1915

Again Force Their Way Into the American Mission and Massacre Christians.

APPEAL SENT TO RUSSIA

But Turkey Has Also Now Promised to "Protect" the Foreigners, and a Clash Might Result.

TIFLIS, Thursday, March 25, (via Petrograd, March 26.)- Turkish troops have committed further acts of violence at the American Mission in Urumiah, Northern Persia, according to a message received by the local Viceroy from Gordon Paddock, the American Consul at Tabriz.

Mr. Paddock transmits a message from Robert M. Labaree, a missionary at Urumiah, to the effect that the Turkish Consul at Urumiah forced his way into the mission compound with a number of Turkish regular troops and removed some Assyrian Christian refugees, who were then massacred.

The Turks also beat and insulted the American missionaries.

Special to The New York Times.

WASHINGTON, March 26.- The American and British Consuls

at Tabriz, Persia, not far from Urumiah, have joined in an appeal to the General commanding the Russian forces there to go to the succor of the American mission at Urumiah, which is besieged by Turkish regular troops and Kurds.

According to press dispatches, a native Bishop and some native Christians have been hanged and an American missionary has been assaulted.

Information of the appeal came to the British Embassy today from the Foreign Office at London, which received a telegram on the subject from the British Consul, telling of the action of himself and his American colleague. Counselor Barclay of the British Embassy laid this information before Secretary Bryan today.

In the dispatch from the British Consul it was said that the Russian General had expressed willingness to proceed to Urumiah if his Government would give him authority to do so. At the same time he expressed the fear that if troops were sent to the scene of the trouble the forces that had been committing indignities at Urumiah might massacre the missionaries and those in their care.

The dispatch from the British Consul, in which the American Consul, Gordon Paddock, joined, was sent from Tabriz several days ago. According to the State Department, nothing in regard to the attacks on American missions has been received by it.

State Department Active.

In view of the alarming press reports of atrocities, including the hanging of sixty men taken from the French Mission and five from the American mission compound at Gulpashan, near Urumiah, the State Department was today stirred to further efforts to obtain protection for the American missionaries and refugees in that vicinity.

Ambassador Morgenthau at Constantinople has been twice appealed to by Secretary Bryan in the last few days to urge the Turkish Government to send protection to the imperiled section, and it was learned tonight that the State Department had received definite assurances from the Turkish Government that protection would be rushed to the scene.

In view of present efforts by the American Government to have Turkish troops sent to the region, it is regarded as probable here that no further effort will be made to get aid from the Russian soldiery. In view of the hostilities between Russia and Turkey, aid from both sides would be impossible. It is suggested also that the Consuls at Tabriz were moved to be cautious in getting troops into the district, for fear that their coming might cause a massacre.

The State Department tonight had received no official notice of the destruction and outrages at Gulpashan, a few miles from Urumiah, as reported to the Presbyterian Board of Foreign Missions.

Everything Being Done, Says Bryan.

"We are not prepared to announce what we May or can do in the matter," said Secretary Bryan, late in the day. He gave assurances, however, that the State Department was doing everything it could. Directions, he said, had been sent to several American Consuls, including Glazebrook at Jerusalem and Paddock at Tabriz, but nothing had been heard from any of the Consuls directly.

Word was received by the British Embassy, as well as the State Department, that the Turkish Government had issued orders for the saving of the Christians.

Additional directions were cabled to Ambassador Morgenthau by the State Department tonight, forwarding the reports received by the Presbyterian Board of Foreign Missions in New York.

The officials fear that the Porte itself can only with difficulty exert control over the irregular Turkish forces reported to be operating in Northern Persia, nominally against the Russians, but also to a larger extent against the native Christians.

Massacre at Gulpashan.

All the men at Gulpashan, a large village near Urumiah, have been shot by Kurds, the women assaulted, an American missionary beaten, and sixty-five refugees, taken from the French and American missions, have been hanged on gibbets erected in the mission yards, according to a cablegram received here yesterday by the Presbyterian Board of Foreign Missions.

The missionary referred to as having been beaten is F. T. Allen, a Canadian, who is a naturalized American.

The sum of $6,000 for relief at Urumiah was cabled yesterday to the American Consul at Tabriz by the Persian War Relief Committee.

This information was contained in a cablegram from Tiflis signed by four native Christians, three of them, and perhaps the fourth, naturalized Americans. The message follows:

Gulpashan destroyed. Its men shot, women violated. Sixty men taken from French Mission compound and five from American Mission compound, hanged. Allen beaten; hanging pole erected in French Mission yard. Massacre imminent. Implore State Department that Consul at Tabriz proceed to Urumiah.

The message was signed by Jesse Yonan, E. O. Eshoo, Isaac Yohannan, and Paul Shimman, all of whom are known to the board. Eshoo and Shimman, both Americans, left this city for Urumiah five weeks ago, proceeding by way of Norway and Petrograd.

Officials of the Presbyterian Board were somewhat surprised yesterday to hear that Secretary of State Bryan had requested the American Consul at Jerusalem to investigate conditions at Urumiah and its vicinity. They said it was almost as difficult to get from Jerusalem to Urumiah as from New York to Urumiah.

"We have requested Secretary Bryan, both by letter and telegram, to do all that is possible to help the situation in Persia," a representative of the board said, "and trust that he will be able to do so through other agencies than the Consul at Jerusalem, who, we understand, would meet great delays and difficulties in going or getting agents to go to Urumiah."

Turkey Promises Aid in Persia – March 28, 1915

Declares Christians Will Be Protected – State Department Still Has No News.

ANXIETY IS NOW LESS

Official of Presbyterian Board of Foreign Missions Regards Situation as More Hopeful.

WASHINGTON, March 27.- Efforts to obtain official information concerning the reported outrages against Americans and refugees in missions in Urumiah and Gulpashan, Northern Persia, were continued today without result. The State Department was bombarded with messages from relatives and friends of Americans believed to be in the disturbed region.

Secretary Bryan, however, received word from Ambassador Morgenthau at Constantinople that the Turkish Grand Vizier had issued orders to his subordinates that all Christians in the danger section be protected and that uprisings be put down.

The state Department was without official information regarding the report that the British and American Consuls at Tabriz, Persia, had petitioned the Russian Government to send

Russian troops from Tiflis to allay the uprising. While it is believed that Russian troops could most expeditiously reach the Urumiah district, it is regarded as unlikely that any will be sent, now that the Turkish Government has agreed to look after the safety of foreigners there.

The American Consul at Tabriz, Gordon Paddock, has been asked to forward all details of the reported atrocities and the whereabouts of persons for whom inquiries have been made.

Many directions, Secretary of State Bryan said today, had gone forward to American diplomatic and Consular officials in the vicinity of the danger zone, urging them to do all they possibly could do.

A communication from the State Department, saying that the Grand Vizier of Turkey had issued instructions to his subordinates that all inhabitants of the mob-ridden section of Persia, including the thousands of Christians in the vicinity of Urumiah, must be protected, was received yesterday by the Presbyterian Board of Foreign Missions.

The communication was signed by Robert Lansing, the Department's Counselor.

"Mr. Lansing advises us," said George T. Scott, assistant secretary of the board, "that Ambassador Morgenthau, at Constantinople, communicated to the Grand Vizier the request of the State Department for the protection of Americans in the vicinity of Urumiah. The Grand Vizier, the letter says, expressed the belief that the reports of outrages there were inaccurate, and told Mr. Morgenthau that he would immediately instruct his subordinates to protect all the inhabitants of the section, including of course, the Christians.

"Mr. Morgenthau's cablegram, the letter said, was dated March 24, but did not reach the State Department until March 26."

Mr. Scott added that the Board was not so apprehensive at present as to the safety of American missionaries in the district as it had previously been. He thought that Mr. Allen, the American missionary, who was beaten by pillaging Kurds, who stormed the American mission, had probably stood guard at the gate to the mission and had received rough treatment because he resisted the mob which was intent upon reaching some of the native refugees inside.

Turkish Concession to US. – March 28, 1915

Further Postponement of the Rules as to Foreign Schools.

CONSTANTINOPLE, March 27.- Through the personal efforts of Henry Morgenthau, the American Ambassador to Turkey, the Council of Ministers has granted a further postponement to next September of the new regulations governing foreign schools in Turkey.

Great satisfaction with this postponement is expressed by the officials of Robert College and the American College for Girls.

Turkish Army Now Due at Urumiah – March 30, 1915

Troops Should Have Been There Last Saturday, Constantinople Says.

WASHINGTON, March 29.- Turkish regular troops were due to arrive last Saturday at Urumiah, Northern Persia, where Americans and other Christians have been attacked by Kurdish bandits, according to official statements made to Ambassador Morgenthau at Constantinople by the Turkish Grand Vizier.

The Ambassador reported this conversation to the State Department today, adding that the Turkish War Office had informed him that "no acts of violence had been committed at Urumiah."

State Department officials noted that the assertions of the Grand Vizier and of the Turkish War Office did not agree with other reports as to the situation at Urumiah. The Grand Vizier said the reported atrocities were "grossly exaggerated," while the War Office denied that there had been any disorders whatever.

The reports of attacks upon foreigners have virtually all come from Tiflis, which is far from Urumiah, and between the two places communication is said to be so difficult that error was to be expected.

It is understood that the Persian Charge here has been endeavoring to obtain definite information without success. However, as the Turkish Grand Vizier assured Mr. Morgenthau that instructions had been sent to the Turkish authorities to suppress any anti-Christian demonstration, and as these instructions are to be supported by the Turkish regular troops, the departmental and diplomatic officials here feel that there is little fear of further attacks, whatever may have happened before the troops arrived.

Mr. Morgenthau reported also that the foreign educational institutions in Turkey had received a further extension of time, until September, before the new instructions of the Turkish Government growing out of the withdrawal last year of the Capitulations guaranteeing extra-territorial rights would be enforced. The American Government protested against that action, as it affected mission schools and colleges at that time. Mr. Morgenthau said the heads of the foreign mission schools hailed the postponement as a victory and were satisfied with the situation.

In making the concession the Turkish Government required that the names of the heads of the various institutions be reported to the public instruction authorities, and Mr. Morgenthau said this order was being compiled with.

In the view of officials here, the enforcement of the new order would virtually end the usefulness of the mission schools, as it would place them directly under Turkish control.

New Promise by Turkey – March 31, 1915

Protection to be Given to the Population of Urumiah, Persia.

WASHINGTON, March 30.- Renewed assurance that protection will be given to the entire population of Urumiah, Persia, where attacks on Americans and other foreigners and on native Christians have been reported, have been given to Ambassador Morgenthau at Constantinople by the Turkish Government.

In a message to the State Department today Mr. Morgenthau said the Ottoman authorities had promised that not only foreigners, but natives as well would be protected by the Turkish regular troops, due at Urumiah last Saturday.

Apparently no advices had been received in Constantinople from Urumiah after the regulars had reached that place as no mention was made of their arrival.

Secretary Bryan recalled the game of gossip today in commenting on the reports from Persia. Tales relayed through many messengers, he said, were certain to be distorted out of all resemblance to the original report, as that pastime of childhood clearly proved. Other officials were also inclined to believe that the Urumiah stories were exaggerated.

Urumiah Physician Here – March 31, 1915

Dr. Yuseff Tells of the Horrors of the Flight from the City.

Dr. A. D. Yuseff, who was attached as a physician to the American Mission at Urumiah, Persia, and who is now in New York, told yesterday of the conditions which have prevailed there since the declaration of the Mohammedan holy war and the beginning of the campaigns of the Kurds from the mountains.

According to Dr. Yuseff, the first inroads of the Kurdish tribes from the mountains to the south of Urumiah took place in October. The people from the neighboring villages took refuge within the walls of the city, the garrison of which was composed of about 3,000 Cossacks, who had been on guard duty there during the three years of the Russian occupation of the district.

Long before their first attack, the Sheikh of the most powerful tribe of the Kurds had made frequent visits to the city at night disguised as a Mohammedan woman and had received accurate information as to the strength of the garrison and its weak points.

Over 3,000 strong, late in October the bandits swept in from the mountains, riding mountain ponies and armed only with axes and long knives.

The attack continued two days and two nights. The safety of the town depended only upon a small number of Russian guns mounted upon the higher buildings and the walls. During the fighting the Kurds were able to approach to within three miles of the walls. Six large villages were razed, and many of the inhabitants who had been unable to flee to Urumiah were massacred.

After the Kurds had been driven off Dr. Yuseff discovered that the bodies of certain Mohammedans who were well known in the town, who had given the Kurds aid in battle, had been hastily buried to conceal the fact that they had taken the part of the enemy while the bodies of the dead Kurds had been left where they had fallen.

In this engagement Dr. Yuseff first saw the flag of the holy war which the Mohammedans carried before them. It was a red hand on a green field, in which the red was the symbol of the power of might, the green the symbol of the power of faith.

At 11:30 on the night of Jan. 2 the people of Urumiah were awaken and warned to flee to the north under the protection of the Cossacks, who were being withdrawn for service in Russia.

Taking only what bread they could find in the house, Dr.

Yuseff and his wife set out, riding one horse, and, with a band of nearly 5,000 Christians, began their flight to safety. On account of the snow and the intense cold, the journey to Julfa, in Russia, took ten days.

Many children and old persons died on the way, and all the refugees suffered the greatest hardships from exposure and hunger. For days their only drinking water was salt water. All along the road they saw evidences of the ravages of the Kurds. In one village a number of little children had been killed and their bodies had been thrown out by the side of the road.

A large number of the inhabitants of Urumiah, however, elected to remain in the town, among them the greater proportion of the staff of the American Mission. It is for the safety of these persons who are relying solely upon the protection of the American flag, that their friends here are at present concerned. According to Dr. Yuseff, at the time of the flight from Urumiah it was an open secret in the town that the Kurdish chieftain had spread the announcement that he would spare the American Mission at all costs.

Two days after the refugees had left Urumiah the Kurds broke into the town, and, as their initial act of war, seventy-five Christians, one of them a Bishop, were hanged.

Dr. and Mrs. Yuseff made their way through Russia under the protection of an emergency passport given to them by the Russian Consul at Khoi, Persia, finally reaching Norway.

Christians in Peril in Urumiah District – April 7, 1915

Turko-German Emissaries Reported to be Active in Rousing and Organizing the Kurds.

JULFA, Province of Erivan, Transcaucasia, Russia, Monday, April 5, (via Petrograd, April 6.)- After several days of investigation in the Urumiah district of Northwestern Persia, a correspondent of The Associated Press made his way to Julfa, over the frontier in Russia, to file this dispatch.

It is the opinion of well-informed observers that the situation of Christians in Urumiah probably will become more dangerous in a fortnight or so. When the rainy season comes to an end, which will be in about two weeks, large movements of Kurdo-Turks are expected, and wandering tribes of Kurds will pour down into the valleys to the west of Lake Urumiah, according to the traditional customs at harvest time. Already there have been some collisions between Kurds and Christians at a point near Kotur, which is to the west of the river.

It is currently reported that Turk-German emissaries have been active in rousing the Kurds.

It is declared with authority in Urumiah that the German Embassy at Teheran has been supplying a German resident of Urumiah with money and instructions how to use it, and a rich Urumian land owner, Medji Sultan, has received 20,000 Turkish pounds (about $90,000) from the Turks.

Want $50,000 for Urumiah – April 10, 1915

Presbyterian Missionaries Need It to Feed 10,000 Refugees.

A fearful rate of mortality among the 10,000 refugees crowded into the yards of the American Mission at Urumiah, where it is said 5,000 persons could scarcely find accommodation, is reported in a communication received here yesterday through the State Department at Washington by the Presbyterian Board of Foreign Missions. So great was the danger of attack, it is said in the communication, that for a while it was unsafe for any one to leave the premises, and consequently the bodies of the dead could not be buried. Later, when the way was opened, one missionary was kept busy attending to the burial of the dead. At times an average of forty refugees died every day.

The communication, which is a copy of one sent to F. W. Smith, American Consul at Tiflis, Transcaucasia, by the Rev. Robert M. Labaree of Urumiah, described in detail the flight of Christians not only from Urumiah, but from all Azerbajan Province, after the withdrawal of the Russian troops, and then continues as follows:

"It is estimated that in all 12,000 took refuge in our mission compounds of Urumiah, while 3,000 more were given shelter at the French Mission. Those who took refuge with us were unharmed, while villages where being plundered and burned, and hundreds of lives were being lost."

Mr. Labaree asks that the Red Cross Society be informed of the plight of the Christians in Urumiah. He has asked the Board of Foreign Missions to furnish the mission with $50,000 for its immediate needs.

Great Exodus of Christians – April 26, 1915

Thousands Suffered Greatest Hardships to Escape Enemies.

DILMAN, Persia, April 24, (via Petrograd to London, April 26.- The exodus of from 20,000 to 30,000 Armenians and Nestorian Christians from Azerbaijan Province, the massacre of over 1,500 of those who were unable to flee, the death from disease of 2,000 in the compounds of the American mission in Urumiah, and possibly of an equal number of refugees in the Caucasus have been confirmed.

When it became known on the night of Jan. 1 and 2 that the Russian forces had left Urumiah about 10,000 Christians fled, most of them without money, bedding, or provisions. Vehicles and camels and donkeys were for hire only at prices at which they might previously have been bought.

A majority of the people started out afoot, through mud knee-deep, across the mountain passes in freezing weather. At Dilman they were joined by many more from Salmas plain. But for Father de Cross of the Roman Catholic Mission at Hosrova, near here, the disaster might have become historic. After assuring the safety of the sisters of the mission, Father de Cross joined the pilgrims and managed to secure bread and shelter for many of them.

The caravansaries were so crowded that few persons could lie down in them, and thousands slept in the mud and the snow. Children were born on the roadside or in the corner of a caravansary.

Arriving at Julfa, on the Russian border, passport difficulties added to the troubles of the fleeing people. Maddened women threw their children into the Araxes River or into pools in order to end their sufferings from cold and hunger.

Father de Cross had to put his back against a wall to fight off the famished mob when he began distributing bread. The mud and cold and the shelterless nights, during which the garments of the refugees were frozen knee high, continued for three weeks, until the people were slowly dispersed by rail. Meantime, hundreds of them had not slept under a roof or near a fire.

Isaac Yonan, a graduate of the Louisville (Ky.) Theological Seminary, was among the refugees. He kept a diary of the happenings during the exodus. This relates that among the refugees from Urumiah were an old man and his two daughters-in-law; with their six children, three of them babes in arms. The oldest child was 9 years old. They were eight days on the way, averaging twenty miles daily through the mud. The old man became stuck fast in a pool and at his own request was left there to die. One woman gave birth to a child during the march and an hour afterward was again plodding along with the other refugees.

Two of the children were lost in a caravansary, but were taken up by Cossacks along with forty other persons. The soldiers displayed great humanity, often giving up their horses to the women.

One young woman carried her father for five days, when he died. A woman was found dead by the roadside with her infant, still living, wrapped up in her clothing.

In a single day twenty persons died in the railway station at Nakhitchevan, across the border in Russia. The entire casualties aggregated hundreds. People died unheeded and unmourned; in fact, those who died seemed to be envied by the living.

Says Turks Aided Recent Massacres – April 29, 1915

Troops Allowed Kurds to Kill Hundreds, American Missionary Reports.

RUSSIA THE SOLE HOPE

Occupation of Persia Alone Can Save Situation, a Missionary Writes.

More than 800 native Christians have been massacred by Kurds, and not less than 2,000 have died of disease at Urumiah, Persia, according to information received by the Presbyterian Board of Foreign Missions yesterday. The Turkish soldiers are accused of aiding or permitting the massacres. Two letters were received from Dr. W. S. Vanneman, head of the Presbyterian Mission Hospital at Tabriz, who is the Chairman of the relief committee appointed by the American Consul. Because of the strict censorship Dr. Vanneman wrote to his wife, who is in Salem, N. J., rather than to the board itself. His letters were sent to the board by Mrs. Vanneman. In a letter of March 14 Dr. Vanneman wrote:

"About ten days ago the Kurds in Salmas, with the permission of the Turkish troops, gathered all the Nestorian and

Armenian men remaining there, it is reported about 800. Four hundred were sent to Khosrova and 400 to Haft Dewan under the pretense of giving them bread. They were held a few days and then all of them tortured and massacred. Many of the women and children were taken away and maltreated. This happened a day or two before the advancing Russian Army took Salmas.

"We are very anxious about Urumiah. A letter dated March 1, from Dr. Shedd (the Rev. Dr. W. A. Shedd of Marietta, Ohio) came through by messenger two days ago. He said things were getting worse. Gulpashan, which hitherto had not been disturbed by the Kurds as it had not fought against them, had been plundered and ruined. I think this was the only village which remained. Fifty-one of the most prominent men of this village were taken out at night to the cemetery and shot. The women and girls who could not escape were violated. This was done by the Turkish soldiers.

"Forty men had been taken from the Roman Catholic Mission, in Urumiah City, kept prisoners a few days, then were taken at night two miles from the city and shot.

"Dr. Shedd asked the American Consul at Tabriz to come to Urumiah, but after consulting with three other Consuls here it was decided it would be impossible to get through. Mr. Paddock has telegraphed every possible place for assistance. We can do nothing more.

"We hear, but do not know if it is true, that the mission in Urumiah has been forced to pay $40,000 as a ransom for the refugees, and we fear it is true. Dr. Shedd writes that not less than 800 had been murdered in Urumiah and not less than 2,000 had died of disease. This applies to Christians only. This is a very large per cent., as more than half of the Christians fled to Russia."

Under date of March 21 Dr. Vanneman wrote:

"We are more anxious than ever about Urumiah. On the 17th Turkish troops attacked our mission and the Roman Catholic Mission and took five native Russian priests from our compound and treated them badly. We do not know yet if they were killed. Mr. Allen was also treated badly because he had sent out three messengers. The gates of the Catholic Mission were burned and they were all in great danger. We received word from Ambassador Morgenthau that orders had been sent to Urumiah to protect Christians, but the order was just too late. We are working to get all the remaining Christians away from Urumiah.

"Some of the native Christian preachers have been crucified and some burned, but these were of other denominations.

"If the Russian troops should be withdrawn again, every Christian would have to leave Tabriz. We have received $6,000 for relief and have spent at least $15,000. If the people have to be moved from Urumiah and then fed, you can imagine what an expense it will be.

"I do not believe the real condition of affairs is comprehended in America. It is practically the extermination of the Syrians (Nestorians) and very bad for the Armenians also. The only hope is occupation by Russia."

Await Expulsion of Kurds – May 2, 1915

Thousands of Christians Want to Return to Persia.

TIFLIS, Transcaucasia, Saturday, March 27, (Correspondence of The Associated Press.)- Many thousands of the Assyrian inhabitants of the country west of Lake Urumiah have had to flee before the coming of the raiding Kurds. Some 45,000 or 50,000 of these people a few months ago occupied the smiling gardens on the lake shores. Now 12,000 are refugees in Russia and some 15,000 or 17,000 took refuge under the protection of the Dr. Harry P. Packard of the American Presbyterian Mission at Urumiah. His successful efforts in their behalf already have been told by cable. His name will survive in Assyrian traditions.

The members of the Central Committee of the Assyrian or Chaldean Christians are awaiting only one thing, the return of the Russians, to endeavor to reconstruct into a safe community this remnant of the ancient empire of Nineveh.

Prof. Yohannan Menaced – May 5, 1915

Arrest of Alleged Agent Follows Threat by Persians.

When the Rev. Dr. Abraham Yohannan, Professor of Oriental Languages in Columbia University, received a letter at his home, 557 West 124th Street, last Friday, written in Persian, the Professor native language, and demanding $200 under threat of death, he carried it to the Fourth Branch Detective Bureau. The letter said the writers wanted to return to Persia and would telephone the Professor, making an appointment to receive the money if he decided to settle with them. Dr. Yohannan was advised to wait for such a message, and Monday he received a second letter telling him the writers hoped he had decided to follow their wishes. Yesterday someone telephoned, and, speaking in Persian, made an appointment to call on the Professor at 10 o'clock last night.

Detectives McManus and Hill were hidden behind some portieres in the library when shortly after 11 o'clock, the maid admitted a young Persian, who afterward said he was Joel Jacobs, 21 years old, employed as an office attendant by Dr. Joseph E. Winters of 25 West Thirty-Seventh Street.

"I presume you come for the money mentioned in the letters I have received?" said the professor.

"I was sent to get some money from you," replied Jacobs. "I know nothing about any letters."

"I promised those men I would give them $100 and pay the rest later," continued the professor, and Jacobs responded: "I guess that will be all right."

Then Dr. Yohannan handed the youth $100 in marked bills, and as he accepted them the detectives seized him. He was apparently greatly astonished and insisted that he had done nothing wrong. He declared he had acted as a messenger for others, but steadfastly declined to say who they were.

Jacobs was locked up, and Dr. Yohannan said he thought the youth, or those he acted for, had conceived their idea from watching moving pictures. He said he did much translating for publishing houses and was well known among the Persians of this city, who doubtless regarded him as wealthy.

Russians Occupy Urumiah – May 29, 1915

Drive Turks from District Where Massacres Took Place.

PETROGRAD, (via London,) May 28. – Urumiah, Persia, has been occupied by the Russians after an engagement with the Turks in the direction of Dilman and near Bachkala, according to a statement issued by the General Staff of the Army of the Caucasus.

Urumiah, in Azerbaijan Province, with a population of about 50,000, is a centre of missionary activity. It is the seat of Fiske Seminary for Girls and of Urumiah College. For weeks the missionaries stationed there, as well as many thousands of Assyrian Christians, have been in grave danger from attack by Kurds and Turks. Between 15,000 and 17,000 natives are reported to have placed themselves under the protection of Dr. Harry P. Packard of the American Presbyterian Mission, at least 12,000 have taken refuge in the Caucasus, and it has been estimated that 20,000 are dead or missing.

The entire Urumiah district has been terrorized by wandering bands of Kurds and by Turkish regulars. Appeals have been made to the American State Department to take measures for the protection of American missionaries, and the Russian Government has been urged to make every effort possible to occupy the district. There have been many reports of atrocities and the wholesale slaughter of natives. The Christians have resisted the attacks of the Kurds as vigorously as possible, but have been handicapped by a lack of guns and ammunition.

Seek Million Names for Peace Petition – July 8, 1915

World's Christian Endeavour Union Also Wants $1,000,000 for Missions.

BEGIN SESSIONS AT CHICAGO

Persian Expresses Gratitude for Protection Against Kurds – German Message Tells of Loss.

CHICAGO, July 7.- "Get a million new members and $1,000,000 for missions," is the slogan of the fifth world's and twenty-seventh international Christian Endeavor Convention, which opened here today.

The call was the subject of an address which was to have been read by the Rev. Francis E. Clark, President and founder of the society. He was unable to be present, however, because of illness.

Delegates were urged to enroll a million new church members, a million signers to a peace petition and a million pledges to make the country a saloonless nation by 1920.

President Wilson sent greetings to the delegates. Explaining his inability to attend, the President wrote:

"My duty becomes more and more clear every day in matters of invitations of all sorts and I feel bound in conscience to address myself without interruption to my public duties here. You could not offer me an audience which would more attract me than the World's Christian Endeavor Union in convention."

The Rev. Francis. E. Clark was re-elected President of the society.

The Rev. Howard B. Cross was elected Vice President; A. J. Shartle, Treasurer; H. N. Lathrop, Clerk; J. J. Arakelyan, Auditor; William Shaw, General Secretary, and Karl Lehmann, Field Secretary. All live in Boston and all are re-elections, except Mr. Lathrop. Selection of a city for the next convention is on the programme for Friday.

The greetings presented by delegates from foreign countries were from India, China, Japan, Germany, Hungary, Spain, Jamaica, Persia, Mexico and Africa.

The message from Persia brought by John B. Keena, who was converted from Mohammedanism by Christian Endeavor missionaries, was one of the most interesting. He said:

"I believe no foreign country represented here tonight has more right to thank this great audience and through this gathering the great American Christian forces, than has Persia.

"The greatest service that America has rendered Persia was performed during the last Winter.

Invaded by the terrible Kurds and everywhere surrounded by the hostile Moslems, the Christians were left to the mercies of the murderers. It became the duty of the American missionaries to undertake the tremendous task of caring for nearly 50,000 refugees. The mission compounds were the only shelter for the natives in their hour of desperation; and the Persian War Relief Committee, headed by Dr. Robert E. Speer, has been and is still doing all in its power to allay the indescribable suffering of those innocent neutral Christians. On the 4th of last January, an American medical missionary from Denver, seeing that nearly 5,000 native Christians were about to be massacred in the village of Googtapa by the onrushing Kurds, flung an American flag high in the air and rode between the battle lines until he reached the Kurdish Chief. The doctor begged this leader of the Moslems to grant him the lives of the innocent Christians. On that day alone, Dr. H. P. Packard of Urmia, Persia, saved 5,000 lives!"

From the heart of the war now raging in Europe the following message was received from the General Secretary, the Rev. Friedrich Blecher of Berlin:

"This war is a mighty summons of God to reflection, so that our members may examine themselves to see whether their conduct is in agreement with their prayers, and therefore at the same time a bowing low in penitence which heals from many faults.

"It is our earnest prayer to God that He by His Holy Spirit will again bring into order what the human spirit has thrown into disorder, and that Christian peoples may become conscious that in spite of all education and culture, 'sin is a reproach to any people,' as this war has revealed in a shocking way."

Daniel A. Poling, Superintendent of the Temperance and Citizenship Department of the society, said in the course of his report:

"We are fully persuaded that the Atlantic City resolution, 'A Saloonless Nation by 1920,' now-the unanimously adopted fighting slogan of the temperance forces, will become a fact of history."

Urumiah Typhoid Victims – July 16, 1915

A Number of the American Mission Colony Have Died.

The Presbyterian Board of Commissioners for Foreign Missions yesterday made public a letter received from Mrs. J. P. Cochran, a mission worker at Urumiah, Northern Persia, written on May 20, a day after the Turks and Kurds left the place because of the approach of superior Russian forces. The letter is addressed to "Friends in America," and describes the sufferings of the people and the missionaries during the occupation of the town by the Turks.

Writing of the scourge of typhoid, Mrs. Cochran says:

"Then we all began to get the typhoid fever. We had some Turkish soldiers in the hospital with it, and the people were ignorant and careless and we had an epidemic. We have seven hundred new-made graves in our compound here at the college as the result of it.

"In the hospital there was a time when the head physician's assistant, Dr. Daniel, who died with it; the matron, druggist, all the nurses, the cook, the bake-woman, the steward, and washer-women were all down together, and two hundred and fifty patients to be taken care of. You can imagine, or rather you can't begin to imagine, the disorganization of the place.

"In the city it was even worse."

Turkish Horrors in Persia – October 11, 1915

American-Educated Native Asks Aid for Thousands of Victims.

Shleeman Malek Yonan, a well-to-do Persian who was graduated from Washington and Lee University in 1913 and returned to his native City of Urumiah, has sent an appeal to the country that gave him his education to help the thousands of sufferers about him.

Mr. Yonan, whose nickname in college was Prince and who as a track athlete established the Washington and Lee record for the broad jump, makes his appeal in a letter written to a classmate on July 25, 1915, in which he describes as much of his terrible experience as the censors would pass. The letter is addressed to F. W. McWaine and has been printed in The Ring-Tum Phi, the Washington and Lee college weekly. It says in part:

"It would take volumes, as big as the Encyclopaedia Britannica to give to the world a picture so horrible. No such thing has happened since Creation.

"When Turkey declared war against the Allies, the Russians, had a small army in Urumiah. A couple of months later the army was withdrawn from Urumiah. Now the sought chance had come to the Mussulmans. Oh, they did what they had contemplated, and a hundred per cent more.

"From that day commenced our tortures and evil days. Honestly, as I am writing, the tears are running down my cheeks. I can't help crying. Thousands and thousands of our people - men, women, and children. have been butchered in cold blood. Thousands of girls from seven years up have been destroyed by the Moslems. Thousands have been forced against their will to become Mohammedans. Our churches are converted into stables - three-fourths of them burned. More than a hundred and twenty villages of Christians have been turned into ashes. Today there is no habitation left for us. Our own houses have been burned - property taken away - absolutely nothing left. Not being satisfied with this, the cruel Moslems imposed a heavy fine upon certain persons. There was a heavy fine on me. I couldn't find the money. Then I was warned to hide myself; if not I would mount the scaffold. I had to borrow the money to pay the fine.

"Well, I suppose you would think perhaps that was enough for me. But this was merely an introduction to the greater horrors. My folks had fled to Russia when they had a chance. My little brother and myself were left behind - found it impossible to go, so we had to stay.

"For exactly four months I hid myself. A Moslem friend of mine hid me. Imagine four months in a dark room, not being able to see even sunlight. Three times I escaped the capture. God himself saved me. The authorities were hunting me hard. Why they were so diligently hunting for me I do not know.

"The Christianity has absolutely perished here. About twelve thousand have perished by famine, murder and typhoid. Thanks to the American missionaries; they did a heroic work. It was their efforts which saved the remaining Christians.

"As a friend, college mate, and classmate, I appeal to you for help. We are making appeals everywhere. The people are starving to death."

In submitting the letter for publication, Mr. McWaine accompanied it with an appeal in Yonan's behalf, saying that contributions might be sent to him, at Lexington, Va., or direct to Shleeman Malek Yonan, Urumiah, Persia.

25,000 Syrians Starving – October 30, 1915

Mountaineers Take Refuge in a Persian Town – Americans Aid Them.

LONDON, Oct. 29.- The Foreign Office has received a dispatch from Mr. Shipley, the British Consul at Tabriz, Persia, which says that 25,000 Syrian mountaineers from the Tyari and adjacent districts have taken refuge in Salmas and that 10,000 more are expected there. All are destitute, and unless help is received many of them will inevitably perish, as Winter is close at hand.

Mr. Shipley adds that the American Relief Committee, under the Presidency of the United States Consul, is endeavoring to do all that is possible, but that its funds are entirely inadequate to meet the requirements of the situation, which justifies an urgent appeal to the charity of Great Britain. Mr. Shipley suggests that all funds be sent to him for distribution through the American Committee, which, he believes, is the best agency for giving effective relief.

Beheaded in Persia – April 16, 1916

Former Student Here is Slain by Turks at Urumiah.

WAUKESHA, Wis., April 15.- Dr. Joseph Shimoon, a former student of Carroll College, Waukesha, and who was a member of the 1903 class of the Jefferson College, Philadelphia, was burned at the stake and beheaded in Persia, according to advices reaching here from Philadelphia.

No date was given in the reports but they show that Dr. Shimoon was seized at Urumiah, Persia, by Turks who tried to compel him to embrace Islamism. Upon his refusal and statement that "Jesus is my Savior," he was seized, set on fire, burned to death and beheaded.

Ask War Relief for the Persians – July 9, 1916

Episcopal Bishops Issue Appeal for Funds for Native Christians.

THREE AMBULANCES SENT

Rockefeller Foundation Gives Another $100,000 for Armenian Red Cross Work.

An appeal signed by some of America's most eminent clergymen has been issued in behalf of the thousands of native Christians in Northwestern Persia and Kurdistan. These people have been reduced to destitution as a result of the war, and since the Russians gained control of the region in which they live it is now possible to get relief to them without very great delay.

This appeal is indorsed and signed by the following Bishops of the Protestant Episcopal Church : David H. Greer and Charles S. Burch of New York, Edwin S. Lines of Newark, James De W. Perry of Rhode Island, Frederick Burgess of Long Island, William Lawrence and Samuel Babcock of Massachusetts, Philip M. Rhinelander and Thomas J. Garland of Pennsylvania, William A. Leonard of Ohio, Richard H. Nelson of Albany, Paul Matthews of New Jersey, C. B. Brewster of Connecticut; Thomas. F. Davies of

Western Massachusetts, and the Rev. Dr. William T. Manning, Rector of Trinity Parish, New York.

The appeal says:

For thirty years the Archbishop of Canterbury's Mission has been at work among the Assyrian (Syrian) Christians in northwestern Persia and Kurdistan. These Nestorians, who have lived near the borders of Turkey and Persia for centuries, have been overwhelmed, since October, 1914, by the suffering of dwellers in a war zone.

The Assyrian Christians are divided into three groups, which have met fates varying with their geographical location. From those on the upper reaches of the Tigris, near Mosul, Turkey, very little has been heard, and the most recent news tells of the massacres of most of those living in the Bohtan region. The second group, inhabiting the plain of Urumia, Persia, has suffered terribly as the tides of war ebbed back and forth over the plain, and many have died through disease, starvation and massacre. The plight of the third main group, which, under the leadership of the Assyrian patriarch, Mar Shimun, fled with great difficulty to the Plain of Salmas in the Autumn of 1915, is even more desperate. In answer to an appeal of the Archbishop of Canterbury, published in The London Times of the 10th of November, 1915, some assistance has been sent from England. Through the American Committee for Armenian and Syrian Relief, with which the Persian War Relief Committee has merged, there has been sent since last November the sum of $115,110. Included in this amount are generous contributions from the Rockefeller Foundation.

It is now increasingly evident that previous efforts at relief have been inadequate. Last Autumn in Persia $10,000, sent by the American Committee for Armenian and Syrian Relief, kept 10,000 persons alive for a month, but this meant rations of bread and salt only.

The latest information from missionary sources and from Mr. Paul Shimmon, personal representative of the Assyrian Patriarch, shows that in spite of all that has been done, exposure, disease, and starvation have cost the lives of a large proportion of the refugees. Thus it is reported in March, 1916, from one locality, that "out of 3,200 refugees in this village 1,000 had already died and there were many who were ill."

Funds are needed at once for clothing and more and better food; also to assist the refugees to render their ruined homes habitable and to plant and harvest crops.

Contributions may be sent to Woodbury G. Langdon, Treasurer of the Assyrian Relief Fund, 30 East Fifty-ninth Street, or to Charles R. Crane, Treasurer of the American Committee for Armenian and Syrian Relief, 70 Fifth Avenue.

The Plight of Assyria – September 18, 1916

Needs of Christian and Kurd in That War-Ravaged Country.

To the Editor of The New York Times.

On July 9 you were very kind to publish in your valued paper an appeal signed by some sixteen prominent Bishops of the Protestant Episcopal Church on behalf of the Assyrian Christians known as Nestorians, or Syrians, living in Northwestern Persia, in Urumia and Salmas, and across the mountains in the heart of Kurdistan. As these noncombatant people have suffered very greatly, even before the regular massacres and deportations of the Armenians in Turkey began, it may interest your readers to hear of their present situation from one than whom no one is better fitted to speak. Dr. H. P. Packard is the head of the American hospital at Urumia. Then his appeal for the Kurds shows his catholic sympathy and generous heart. It may be recalled that Dr. Packard with two Syrian doctors - both of whom have since fallen victims to typhoid - risked their lives and saved some 2,000 souls in Geogtapa, five miles from Urumia, when he pleaded their cause with the Kurd who was attacking the town and took them at night to the city, when Geogtapa was given to the flames and entirely plundered.

I have added in parentheses some explanatory notes to show the various phases that may help to make the letter more vivid.

PAUL SHIMMON,
Representing Mar Shimun, Patriarch of the Syrian Church.
New York, Sept. 15, 1916.

Letter from Dr. H. P. Packard, Urumia, Persia, dated July 21, 1916.

Relief burdens are still heavy, and it is hard to know what is the least that we can do for the sake of the Christians. You know from personal experience how hard it is to get the Moslem masters (who, as a rule, own the land on which Christians live) to do anything for their Christian subjects. We do not want to use relief money for the advantage of these masters, but it may be that in many cases Christians cannot get any help from their masters to re-roof their homes, and may have to sit in ruins if we do not do something for them. (The village masters, as a rule, have also been hardly knocked by the war.) It may be that by giving part of the timber we may be able to induce masters to supply the remainder. We sincerely hope that there will not have to be as much crowding during the coming Winter as there was in the past. (It is the third

Winter in Urumia and Salmas since they were destroyed.) Some of the villages, such as Balou, Gachen, Walinda, and Geogtapa, have been terribly crowded with the people of Tergawar, Dasht, and Mergawar, (districts on the Perso-Turkish border which had been destroyed even before the war began,) besides many from Mar-bishoo and Nochea, (Turkish frontier,) as well as some from Tiari and other places in the mountains over the border. The Matran (Metropolitan Bishop of the Nestorian Church living in Nichea, Turkey, near the border,) has gone to Umbi, in Tergawar, and is now sitting there, and others are beginning to push up toward the foothills, but I fear that there will be no earnest effort to get these people established for the Winter, and we may expect them to return to the plain, even if peace should be declared in the Fall. (This was written before they knew anything of what was to happen in Bitlis and Mush, in Armenia, which fell into Turkish hands in August, although since then retaken for the fourth time by the Russians.) Their villages are entirely in ruins, and there is no timber to be found without taking it from the Urumia plain, and the scarcity of cattle will make it impossible to accomplish this work this Autumn, even if it were considered safe for the people to go back now, and we cannot get this assurance from the authorities. Some movement has begun toward Bashkala, (on the Turkish, border,) but it promises to be small, and the investigation made in the mountains by David, the brother of Mar Shimun, and Malick Khoshaaba and Malick Ismael, and their men makes them feel that there is no hope of getting back to their homes before Winter. This means that the mountaineers (the bulk of the Nestorian Church) will be on us for another Winter, and that relief work in Urumia will be heavy for some time. These mountaineers have had no fields to sow; they have no harvest. They have had to depend on charity so far, and will have to depend on relief until they can return to their homes.

We already have begun to make quilts. We shall make 2,000 now and 2,000 or 3,000 in the Fall if we see that there is need for them. We have also arranged to spend $3,000 for simple garments to be ready for the late Fall. I succeeded in concluding the first wheat purchase today. We got fifty loads at 65 krans, (about $8 now,) and have had 200 loads offered in Dole for 60 krans per load. The crops are small here, and we expect that prices will be high this year, for there was no sowing in Tergawar, Dasht, or Mergawar, and the Sulduz sowing was much less than usual, and much of the young wheat has been pastured. The Enzel crop is about half of the normal, and Somai also cannot furnish much for outside. (These are fertile districts in noncombatant Persia, but crushed by war conditions.)

One of the greatest needs of the present time is that among the Kurds. I realize that this question will not be popular with many Christians in America, as well as in Persia. The Begzadi Kurds who are left on this side of the border are rayats (subjects) and not servants of the chiefs, who are the riflemen. We all know that when fortune favors them these rayats are almost as predatory as the servant class, but when the servants ran off with the chiefs they stripped the rayats of everything that they could take away, and we see these people starving now. They have nothing to reap for the coming year, so their condition is far more deplorable than that of the Christians. There will be few to appeal for the Kurds, but this is an opportunity that Christendom is not likely to have again. If we would follow the teachings of the Christ whom we profess to follow we would pray more for these same Kurds than we have, and we should be glad in this time of their great need to give to them and show them that the Masters teaching is different from that of their prophet. (These Kurds are to the Christians in Persia what the Mexican bandits are to the Americans, with the further difference that Persia is even far worse than Mexico, and Christians are not on the same level with Mohammedans before the courts, &c.)

Our reports for work till July 1 will contain estimates of the needs, of the coming Winter, because supplies should be laid in now if we would get them as economically as possible, and it is necessary that we should have large sums of money soon. The quilt business here and in Salmas will consume $30,000, and the clothing account will require an expenditure of not less than $8,000. The wheat bill for the year we cannot estimate accurately yet. But I think we shall have to spend not less than $100,000 before another harvest.

Asks for $5,000,000 to Succor Armenia – October 4, 1916

American Committee Starts Biggest Undertaking of Mercy Since Relief of Belgium.

WASHINGTON, Oct. 8.- The greatest American Relief Campaign to be undertaken since organization of the Belgian Relief Commission was launched today by the American Committee for Armenian and Syrian Relief. An exhaustive summary of the whole Armenian and Syrian situation was made public and will be sent to ministers of 120,000 churches all over the country and to many leading citizens and relief organizations.

A fund of $5,000,000 is called for to relieve 1,000,000 destitute, exiled and starving Armenians and Syrians scattered broadcast over Turkey, Persia, Syria and Palestine. The appeal declares that of nearly 2,000,000 Armenians originally in their native country, three-quarters of a million have been massacred or have died of wounds, disease or exhaustion since the war began.

The allied blockade has been lifted to allow passage of the supplies. Oct. 21 and 22 have been set aside by proclamation by President Wilson as relief days.

"People were found eating grass, herbs, and locusts," says the committee in describing its investigation of conditions in Armenia, "and in desperate cases dead animals and human bodies are reported to have been eaten. In some cases men were lined up so that several could be shot with one bullet in order not to waste ammunition. A mother said that not a girl above 12 (and some younger) in the village of -------- escaped violation. The people kill and eat the street dogs. A short time ago they killed and ate a dying man.

"Of 450 from one village only one woman lives. She saw her husband and three sons tied together and shot with one bullet to save ammunition. She saw her daughter outraged and then killed. She was carried away by a Kurd but escaped by night, naked, and after terrible suffering fell in with some refugees.

"In the literal sense of the word, 100,000 to 120,000 Armenians arrived at Etchmiadzin, stripped even of their outer garments. There 11,000 died and 40,000 more in the country.

Bishops Appeal for Nestorians – November 13, 1916

Ask American Aid for 100,000 Christians Who Are Victims of Moslems.

ARE DYING OF STARVATION

Their Plight Parallels That of the Serbs and Armenians, Bishop Greer's Committee Reports.

Sixteen bishops of the Protestant Episcopal Church in the United States issued an appeal yesterday on behalf of a group of Nestorian Christians of Assyria. Headed by Bishop Greer of New York the bishops who signed the appeal bring for the first time, it is stated, to the attention of the people of this country, the story of the battle for life on the plains of Kurdistan of an entire people, a struggle which the bishops add "went on practically without the knowledge of Europe or America, and which ended in the complete destruction of 1,000 Christian tribesmen and the reduction to destitution of 100,000 more."

The appeal continues:

"The Assyrian Christians are of Syriac origin and are related racially to the Syrians. For centuries they have lived along the borders of Turkey, Persia and

Russia, chiefly in the high ranges to the east of the Tigris Valley and north of Arabia. At the beginning of the war, according to the first news of any completeness which is just reaching America through missionary sources, the Turks and the Kurdish tribes in Persia attacked the Assyrian Christians without warning. These latter, most of them herdsmen and farmers of sturdy stock and persistent traditions, were able in some cases to retreat to plateau fastnesses, selling their lives as dearly as possible, but falling to protect their families from the brutality of the Kurds and the lower class Turks.

"While the world was watching the more spectacular fortunes of war in Western Europe and along the Russian front an epic that took place on the heights of Eastern Asia, as full of dramatic incidents and heroic fighting against odds, perhaps, as has ever occurred. The fragmentary accounts of this struggle, which was protracted for months, now reaching this country and England, indicate that when the full story is known the tragic history of Serbians and Armenians will be found to have been duplicated in a region entirely out of the main path of the world war.

"The most significant fact brought out in these reports concerns the needs of 100,000 refugees, chiefly women and children who, left to die by the Kurds and Turks, have struggled together in pittably desperate bands to the lower villages of Kurdistan, where they are cared for by Russian and American and in some spots German relief agencies. These agencies have sent appeals which have reached the American Committee for Armenian and Syrian relief, at 70 Fifth Avenue, which has undertaken to send supplies. Already more than $115,000 has been sent. A large share of this has been contributed by the Rockefeller Foundation, and most of it has sought rations of bread and salt for thousands of refugees.

"Another letter says: 'Christians are living in barns and stables. They are so lean and emaciated that death will get at them wholesale.'

"One of the letters from Asia Minor on which the bishops have their appeal says: 'These people are dying for actual lack of nourishment. Those who are sick and those who are well are all huddled together under a few quilts. In some cases the wife or the daughter buries the family dead. Many of them are so lightly covered that very soon the dogs get them out.'"

The appeal of the bishops, which relates further details of the condition of the refugees, is signed by:

David H. Greer, Bishop of New York; Charles S. Burch,

Suffragan Bishop of New York; James De Wolf Perry Jr., Bishop of Rhode Island; William Lawrence, Bishop of Massachusetts; Samuel G. Babcock, Suffragan Bishop of Massachusetts; Frederick Burgess, Bishop of Long Island; Philip M. Rhinelander, Bishop of Pennsylvania; Thomas J. Garland, Suffragan Bishop of Pennsylvania; William T. Manning, Rector of Trinity Parish New York; Edwin S. Lines, Bishop of Newark; Chauncey B. Brewater, Bishop of Connecticut; Thomas F. Davies, Bishop of Western Massachusetts; William A. Leonard, Bishop of Ohio; Charles T. Olmsted, Bishop of Central New York; Richard H. Nelson, Bishop of Albany; W. R. Stearly, Suffragan Bishop of Newark, and Paul Matthews, Bishop of New Jersey.

New Plea for Armenians – August 10, 1917

U.S. Consul at Tiflis Says 350,000 Need $500,000 a Month.

A cable dispatch from the American Consul at Tiflis, disclosing the increasing misery of hundreds of thousands of Armenian and Syrian refugees in the Caucasus and Eastern Turkey, was made public yesterday by the American Committee for Armenian and Syrian Relief. It follows:

"Estimates place the number of Armenian and Syrian refugees in the Caucasus at 250,000, and in Eastern Turkey at 100,000. The total is being slowly increased by newcomers. Of these 250,000 are without employment. A large proportion of them are women and children. Our committee is anxious to help these. The minimum estimate necessary for each individual is $3 per month. In order to meet the needs of the situation the minimum estimate is $500,000 per month.

"I strongly urge the need of support of fatherless children. Of these 5,000 are now on our list, and about 15,000 others require immediate help. No funds are available at present for this department.

"The medical department is caring for many old and sick and for babies. The need is great in other centres. Send new workers at once as follows: One doctor, two women for orphanage, one man, well trained, for leader of technical industrial work, and three or four general workers.

"We urge that not less than the following sums be sent immediately for the departments indicated: Repatriation, $1,000,000; fatherless children in homes, $500,000; industrial relief, $500,000; animals, $150,000; orphanages, $100,000; medical relief, $100,00; seed, $100,000. Machines, looms, and engines for weaving wool would greatly help to meet the needs of the coming Winter and be of permanent value in establishing the industry."

Persia Starts Parley – January 7, 1918

Wants Both Russians and Turks to Evacuate Country.

PETROGRAD, Jan. 4, (Associated Press,) – The Persian Charge d'Affaires today advised Leon Trotzky, the Bolshevist Foreign Minister, that the Persian Government had instructed him to open immediate negotiations with the authorities of the Smolny Institute, the headquarters of the Bolsheviki, for the evacuation of Persia by the Russians.

The Persian note said instructions had also been sent to the Persian Legation at Constantinople for the commencement of negotiations for the evacuation of Persia by the Turks.

Trouble for the Levant – January 15, 1918

With Russia Out, Christian Races Will Be In Great Danger.

To the Editor of The New York Times.

If the present negotiations between the Bolsheviki and the Central Powers to make peace on the basis of 'no indemnities and no annexations", are successful, what will be the effect on the "Eastern question"- the treatment of the non-Moslems by Moslem Governments-and under whose control will those countries pass in the immediate future?

Suppose that the Russians withdrew their troops from Turkey. The occupied territory would at once revert to the Turks again. There is no such place as "Armenia" inhabited exclusively by the Armenians. In none of the six "Armenian vilayets" bordering on Russia and Persia would the Armenians be in the majority. So even the farce of a self-determination by the Christians could not be attempted. Further, the conditions would be worse than before the war, due to bitter enmity engendered by the war, enormous loss of man power, ruined homes and business, and a Turkish Armenia resubjugated.

Turning to the Assyrians, (Nestorian Syrians,) &c., living on the Persian-Turkish borderland, the situation is even more disheartening. The bulk of the independent "tribes" of Mar Shimun, their chief, after fierce struggles for existence, fled to northern Persia. Whatever is left of them now are in Persia, a burden on the land and on themselves, with no prospect of self-support during the war, impoverished beyond description, decimated; but still their men are at the forefront of the Russians leading toward Mosul to make a junction with the English forces in Mesopotamia. Now it is proposed by the Germans that both Russians and Turks (the latter for the sake of appearance) withdraw from Persia and leave the country to decide its own destiny, unmolested from outside interference. On the surface a very unselfish motive indeed. But what does it mean? In the first place, as touching the temporary welfare of the Mountain Assyrians, they would be driven out of Persia. The Persian do not want them in their country. They have shown no pity to their own fellow Moslems in deep distress, whom the American Red Cross is keeping alive, much less to those deported (rather imported) Christians. The Christians are kept where they are by the Russian army, to whom they owe their existence. The Kurd is now hungry and meek, but as soon as he is fed he will be a wolf again (and "Kurd" means

68

"wolf.") These Christians cannot return to their former homes, in absolute ruin, under their present condition. Their doom is certain.

But the evacuation of Persia by Russia has a far larger significance. Russia is weak. Russia will remain weak for years to come. She will be busied with internal matters for years. She may even be broken up into smaller governments. She will have ceased to be the terror-inspiring neighbor to Turkey and Persia, and she will not be able to finance Persia to the extent she has done in the past. But Persia also is weak and cannot finance herself. She has no money, no enterprise, and no resources. The attempt at a revolution has not brought the unification desired - the country did not seem ready for such changes as yet. So Persia must be financed and guided from outside for many years to come. Who will replace Russia in the council of Persia? The great anxiety of Potsdam for Persia is not on humanitarian principles for poor benighted Persia. It is only another name for a clean sweep for a Middle Europe, with its ramifications reaching from the Baltic to the Black and Caspian seas, to include, among others at the Bagdad end of the plan, Persia, Turkey, and Arabia.

PAUL SHIMMON.
Representative Patriarch Assyrian People. New York, Jan. 13, 1918.

Call for Clothing for War Sufferers – March 24, 1918

Armenian and Syrian Relief.

The American Committee for Armenian and Syrian Relief, 1 Madison Avenue, has received from one of its representatives in the Near East a letter telling of the conditions existing in Persia. In part this letter reads:

In the whole of the Province of Adzerbaijan, the greatest and richest in all Persia, the crops were less than half an ordinary crop. The bulk of the people we are helping get nothing in the way of food but dry bread.

An old woman, a good old friend of mine since years before the war and one who was in excellent circumstances, said to me the other day: "Sahib, the bread won't go down. I soak it in water, but it sticks in my throat. I have sold all I have but the vineyard and no one will buy that. I have gone everywhere, but no one has money to lend." These people haven't even the satisfaction of being deported by the military and fed while making munitions to be fired against their friends. They would gladly be taken prisoners and deported - if fed.

They are hungry and dying. Just now a case came interrupting me in my writing. A Jewish woman says a Syrian (Christian) woman came to her house begging late in the evening. Being late, she was allowed to spend the night in a corner of the house and this morning was found dead. She says to me: "Will you please send someone to bury her?" Such pleas are frequent now. This morning I was stopped in the yard by an old man who said: "Sahib, there is a dead man in our yard; please send some one to take him away." There are more dead than are buried. Men and women, once in good circumstances, self-respecting and respected by others, now hungry, helpless, and friendless, crawl away out of sight; die unseen, and lie unburied. This is not fiction; l have seen them.

Even should the war end in the near future, we shall have to continue relief work in bulk over the Winter of 1918 and 1919, and in a smaller degree for some years to come. The people of all classes are impoverished, the supplies of the country are exhausted, the trade of the country has disappeared; the farming cattle have diminished alarmingly; recuperation, therefore, will be long and tedious. We have already given out something over 30,000 pood of Fall wheat, (over 18,000 bushels.)

Cleveland, H. Dodge; Treasurer of the Armenian and Syrian Relief Committee, acknowledges recent gifts to the fund which total more than $300,000. The total contributed to the fund, since organization more than three years ago, now amounts to more than $9,000,000. The new contributions include subscriptions from Sunday school children in Japan, Brazil, and Egypt.

Among the donations of $100 or more are the following:

American Red Cross..........$200,000
Sunday schools........................26,500
Mrs. S. V. Harkness 5,000
Edward S. Harkness..................5,000
Philadelphia citizens.................3,000
New York City citizens.............4,000
Minneapolis citizens................1,000
Capital District Com., N.Y........2,000
Paterson Committee.................1,000
New Britain Committee...........1,191
Egyptian Sunday schools........2,000
Miss Edna E. Hughes....................500
E1izabeth citizens.........................500
Japanese Sunday schools............200
Brazil Sunday schools..................200

Murder of Mar Shimun – April 15, 1918

Syrian Catholicos First Head of a Nationality to Perish in the War.

The American Committee for Armenian and Syrian Relief last night gave out the following concerning Mar Shimun, head of the Assyrian Church, who was killed recently, according to a cablegram received by the State Department at Washington on Saturday.

Mar Shimun is the first political head of a nationality who has paid the supreme sacrifice of this war. To his people he was both King Albert and Cardinal Mercier. In 1903, when a boy of 16, Mar Shimun was selected to become Catholicos or Patriarch, to succeed his uncle, Ruwel Reuben, who was on the point of death. He was consecrated Catholicos on April 12 of that year. He was educated by native teachers and by members of the mission established by Archbishop Benson of Canterbury at the Patriarchal seat, Qudshants, (Kochannes,) in Kurdistan.

His elder sister, Surma, who ranked next to him in influence over his people, also was educated at the mission and later became a recognized authority on canon law and Church history.

Attacked by the Turks in June, 1915, Mar Shimun and his 125,000 Assyrian highlanders defended the narrow valley of their mountain home, which might be termed a Switzerland in Asia. After Turkish mountain guns had battered down ancient castles and churches, the Assyrians were forced to abandon their valley and retreat to mountain fastnesses.

When their supplies ran out, Mar Shimun, with a handful of warriors, risked great perils to reach the Russian lines at Salmas, Persia, but the Russians, weakened by the loss of Warsaw, could give no assistance. Then Mar Shimun, returning to his people, was forced to lead them down to the plateaus of Northwestern Persia, where they scattered over the plains of Salmas and Urumiah. There 15 per cent. of them died from cold and hunger.

As 138th Catholicos of the east he maintained the ancient traditions and his people almost worshipped him.

Turks Killing Americans? – April 29, 1918

Athens Hears of Slaughter of Missionaries in the Caucasus.

Special Cable to THE NEW YORK TIMES.

ATHENS, April 28, (Dispatch to The London Times.) – Trustworthy information has been received here to the effect that the Turks advancing in the Caucasus are compassing the wholesale massacre of Christians and killing indiscriminately Armenians, Greeks, and even American missionaries.

Turks Occupy Tabriz, Second Persian City – June 18, 1918

In Order to Protect Their Caucasian Front, Says an Official Statement.

LONDON, June 17.- Turkish troops have occupied Tabriz, next to Teheran the largest city in Persia, according to a Turkish official statement dated June 14.

The text reads:

We have occupied both shores at Lake Urumiah and the town of Tabriz (Northwestern Persia) in order to protect the wing of our army on the Caucasian front.

MOSCOW, June 4, (Associated Press.)- Turkey having reached an understanding with the leaders in the Transcaucasian District, there are indications that the Ottoman troops will not encounter any further opposition in that section and May move freely toward the Port of Baku, on the Caspian Sea.

The Transcaucasian Government with which Turkey treated fell to pieces after the agreement was reached, but the dismembered sections are friendly to Turkey.

Once at Baku the Turks, in the opinion of observers here, would have easy access to and across the Caspian to Turkestan and could reach the great cotton stores there. Alexandropol is connected by rail with Baku through Tiflis, the capital of Georgia. As Georgia is now friendly to the Turks, there apparently will be no hindrance to their movements along the 300 miles of railroad between Alexandropol and Baku.

Tabriz is in the centre of the former Russian sphere of influence in Northern Persia, halfway between the Caspian Sea and the Persian-Armenian line. Lake Urumiah is halfway between the town and the frontier. The town, formerly a great trade centre, still has a population of 175,000. It is situated on a plateau at an altitude of 4,500 feet, and is the capital of the Province of Azerbaijan. It is 300 miles south of the Caucasus town of Tiflis; and 430 miles northwest of Teheran. The lake has a water area of 1,795 square miles, and is more of a drowned land than a lake - so shallow that mosquitos are said to have no difficulty in wading across.

Since the withdrawal of the Russian Army of the Caucasus the Turks in Armenia. have been opposed only by Cossack detachments, and, in isolated columns, or bands, have been gradually working southeast from the old front, Trezizond - Erzerum - Lake Van, so as to join forces with the armies driven north in the direction of Mosul, on the Tigris, by General Marshall and his Anglo-Indian troops operating in Mesopotamia. At last accounts Marshall was sixty miles south of Mosul. The left Turkish wing on Lake Urumiah and at Tabriz is 200 miles northeast of that place.

Suicide Laid to Slanders – August 15, 1918

Charges Against Consul Baaba Led to Death of His Wife.

CHICAGO, Aug. 14. – A Coroner's jury today decided that the suicide here yesterday of Mrs. Sargis Baaba, wife of the Persian Consul at Chicago, was due to worry over investigation of charges against her husband.

The charges that Baaba had assisted Persians and Syrians to evade the draft are said to have been without foundation, but were made the basis of attacks by Baaba's compatriots, which greatly worried Mrs. Baaba.

The Consul, who is a naturalized American, has been in Washington for several weeks.

Assyrians Not Syrians – August 17, 1918

To the Editor of The New York Times:

In a Chicago dispatch that appeared in your columns this morning the statement was made that the Persian Consul, according to certain charges, helped Persians and "Syrians" to evade the draft. No Persian Consul in the United States could have anything whatever to do with the Syrians, whose interests since the severance of diplomatic relations with Turkey have been in the hands of the Spanish Embassy and Consulates. Evidently the reference is not to Syrians, but to Assyrians, who come from the northwestern part of Persia, and would naturally come within the scope of the Persian Consul's activity. Failure to keep clear the distinction between Assyrians and Syrians has often led to great confusion.

PHILIP K. HITTI.
Columbia University, Aug. 15, 1918.

Persian Armenia Ravaged by Turks – October 11, 1918

Massacre at Urumiah – 47,000 Refugees Reach British Lines in Mesopotamia.

LONDON, Oct. 10.- Mesopotamian dispatches received here record the arrival inside the British lines of 47,000 Assyrian, Armenian, and Russian refugees from Urumiah, Persian Armenia, who broke through the Turkish front and made their escape.

Another 10,000 refugees, according to the dispatches, are distributed in Kurdistan towns or are wandering in the hills. The Turks pursued them, but were driven back by British cavalry.

Later the Turks entered Urumiah and massacred 200 persons, mostly old men. It is reported that 600 Christian women have been distributed among the Turkish troops and the Moslem inhabitants of Urumiah.

Magnitude of Mesopotamian Campaign – October 20, 1918

Lieut. Col. Milne Points Out Importance of the Capture of Bagdad and Subsequent Operations – He Discusses the Remarkable Baku Expedition

In the Occidental mind Haroun-Al-Rashid's importance as a fictional figure overshadows his historic status. All of us remember that the Caliph liked to look on incognito at the procession of his life in the capital. How many of us remember that he was monarch of an empire stretching from Spain to China, the fabulous cradle of world wealth and culture? And how many of us have reflected that Germany's dream of such another empire was a factor in this war, with German trade methods and German Kultur as its backbone?

That dream of empire was not merely a factor, but the immediate cause of the war, in the opinion of Lieut. Col. J. S. Wardlaw Milne, who has played an important part in the British Mesopotamian campaign and who was in New York recently. He regards the campaign as of equal importance with the Western front and the capture of Bagdad as a crushing blow to German ambitions.

"Whatever Germany does in the way of restitution and reparation in France and Belgium," he observed, "if she leaves the peace table in possession of Mesopotamia and the road open to the East she will have won this war."

General Allenby's great successes in Palestine, although spectacular and valuable, are inferior in importance to the achievements of near by in the Bagdad campaign, in Colonel Milne's opinion; and he was emphatic in refuting the ill-informed theory that the two campaigns are one, or have any immediate vital bearing on one another.

When the Colonel spoke the latest news from Mesopotamia had been a meager bulletin from about the British evacuation of Baku. He knew no more about the Baku expedition from official sources than do you, but his familiarity with the territory over which the campaign is being waged was such that he was able to construct an interesting hypothesis of what had happened.

"When the story of that expedition finally comes to be known," he said, "undoubtedly it will be the most thrilling in the war. Not more than a handful of men could have taken part in it. They must have fought their way across 600 miles of Persia, a vast interior infested by robber bands, until they reached Enzeli on the Caspian Sea. There they made their way by boat to Baku, hoping to organize the Armenians against the Central Powers.

"You must not suppose the Armenian cannot fight. He can. He has proved it before now. I hold no brief for that nation, although I do feel heartily sorry for it. I confess even to some repugnance personally toward Armenians, but I admit that they can fight. And so I think the purpose of this amazing expedition was to enlist the considerable Transcaucasian Armenian forces against the Turks. Apparently that intention was not fulfilled. If it had been fulfilled it would have put an end to the German hope of a road through Batum and Baku to the East.

"For Germany, having sold out for the promise of the Berlin-to-Bagdad road, and then having found herself balked by the fall of Bagdad, turned naturally toward the Batum-Baku road. That way lies the path to Peking. Upon the Mesopotamian campaign now, and upon the steadfast purpose of the Allies when the time comes to talk of peace, depends the question whether Germany's plan for a conquest of the East is to be realized.

"Few persons realize the magnitude of the Bagdad campaign. I am not at liberty to tell the number of men engaged in it, but I can at least say that the number cannot be expressed in tens of thousands nor in hundreds of thousands. Lieutenant General Sir John Marshall is now maintaining a line of communication with his base more than 700 miles long, and supplies are transported by boat along the Tigris River. His forces are in three sections. One arm is stretched forward along the Euphrates River, through the region of the Garden of Eden, to a point somewhere west of Hit. The central arm, of which he is in command, is east of the Tigris, about sixty miles south of Mosul. The eastern arm is thrust along the borders of Persia, and it was from this force, I assume, that the expedition was sent to Baku.

"A line from Hit north to Mosul and thence east to the Persian frontier will show graphically what these forces have done to wreck the German hope of dominion in the Near East. We hear little or nothing about it now because from May to October the heat makes extensive operations impossible.

"The work done by these forces is not only military, but reconstructive. They have reclaimed 1,100 square miles of land, have irrigated it and put it under cultivation, and are now producing food in such volume as to save 2,000,000 tons of shipping annually for the Allies. The Sha'albah bund, or river wall, near Basra, is forty feet thick at the bottom, seven feet high, and eleven miles long; but that piece of engineering covers but a pin's head in that vast and fertile country.

"It is a country without wood or stone. The British forces have had to import even their firewood. Under the dominion of the Turk what was once a garden spot of the world had become a wasted ruin, and it is necessary to irrigate the land before it can be made productive. With irrigation nearly anything can be grown there. The work being done is so extensive, and the number of men required so great, that there are Generals in Mesopotamia who have never heard the sound of a gun there. The transport problem is tremendous. It involves 2,000 boats of shallow draught for the Tigris River alone-2,000 boats under Government control, aside from the native craft.

The common impression that the Palestine and Mesopotamian campaigns are halves of a whole is a mistake. They do affect one another, but they have different objectives, and there seems no intention now of linking them. The forces under General Marshall are advancing due north. If they were to follow the Euphrates River northwest as far as Aleppo, it is possible that the forces under General Allenby, pushing forward from Jerusalem, might join them there; but at present there seems no indication that such is the intention."

Lieut. Col. Milne, whose regiment was stationed at Bombay, was detached to serve as an adviser in the Mesopotamian transport problem, and organized the transport from Basra to India and Great Britain for the successful second campaign which resulted in the fall of Bagdad. The transport from Basra into the interior, along the Tigris, was in other hands; but Colonel Milne, although he himself disclaims any part in it, is said to have been requisitioned for service in that branch of transport too. He was with General Maude until three days before that officer's death from cholera. He spoke of the General's death as the greatest loss England had suffered in the Mesopotamian campaign.

When asked to explain his statement that Germany had "sold out" for the promise of the Berlin-to-Bagdad road, Colonel Milne said:

"Germany accepted that bribe in 1897. The European powers were attempting to bring pressure on Turkey to stop the Armenian atrocities. Germany alone stood aside, and we now know that her reason for silence was that she was bought with the great concession of the Bagdad railway. That scheme, with its forest and mining rights, and other concessions Germany had in view, was intended not only to give her control of the Turkish Empire, but to bring the whole area from the North Sea to the Indian coast under the Kaiser's sway.

"With the taking of this bribe arose a dream of empire which was to give her naval control of the Mediterranean, on the one hand, and of the Persian Gulf and Arabian Sea, on the other. With the preaching of a 'Jehad,' or holy war, the Arab was to rise at the call of his co-religionists in Constantinople, and with hordes of barbarian soldiery at her command, Germany was to thrust the British out of Egypt and India, large portions of Russia were to be brought under her control, a new empire with its capital at Bagdad was to be established, and German influence and power were to extend without opposition or hindrance from Hamburg to Singapore.

"As a result of the Balkan wars there arose one barrier across this line, the little country of Serbia. But with the deepening of the Kiel Canal, and the termination of long preparations at home, the appearance of possible civil war in England and the hope of an uprising in India, everything pointed to the day having arrived. The hour had struck, an excuse was found to crush Serbia, and thus the great war began.

"While it is probably true that these dreams of empire were not realized in pre-war days as they are today, enough of

Germany's plan in the East was known to make it absolutely essential that she be immediately checkmated in the event of her being successful in dragging Turkey into the war. When, therefore, in October, 1914, war with Turkey could no longer be avoided, the British had to face the necessity of sending an expeditionary force to Mesopotamia to build a barrier across Germany's line of advance to the East.

"It was in the nature of things that this force should come from India, which had already been bled white to provide men and materials for the western front. It will not be possible until after the war to publish a full statement of the efforts made by India to support the mother country. From Rajah to Ryot all united to send help to Europe, and the call for men and money met with a wonderful response throughout the length and breadth of India. And, when the necessity for action in Mesopotamia arose, the further need had to be met from India, and although ill-equipped for the task and on a very small scale, the small force lying on transports in the Persian Gulf was landed in November, 1914, at the mouth of the Shatt-'al-Arab, (the name given to the confluence of the two rivers Tigris and Euphrates,) and in the following month Bosra, the Port of Mesopotamia, famous as the spot from which Sinbad the Sailor embarked on his memorable voyages, was captured by the British.

"The activity of the Turks, reinforced from Bagdad and the constant attempts of the Germans to stir up trouble in Persia, made an advance to the north by the means of the River Tigris, essential, and, after hard fighting and terrible privations, Qurna was occupied in April, 1915. The horrors of this campaign are little realized in the allied countries even today. Ill-equipped in almost every respect, ill-supplied with everything required to make a campaign successful, fighting in a country with no resources of its own and hundreds of miles from its base, the British expeditionary force had to push further and further north, contending with every possible privation, with unique and terrible heat, with almost every insect pest known, and fighting and dying in a land without sanitation and without any of the necessities and surroundings which go to make life worth living.

"After a wonderful march in the hottest time of the year, the town of Amara, on the River Tigris, was captured in June, 1915, and the British forces pushed on to Kut-el-Amara, and then to Ctesiphon, only a short distance southeast of Bagdad. The question of attempting any further advance was a matter for very careful consideration. On the one hand was the fact that the force was already several hundred miles from its base, that it had never been expected or hoped that it could push so far in so short a time and that it would be in great danger if it met with more serious resistance.

"On the other hand, there was the possibility of the capture of Bagdad, not only in itself desirable as a marked victory for the Allies, but of the greatest political importance, if it could be achieved, in securing the loyalty and good-will of a large number of Mahommedans and of several of the more important Arab tribes. There was also the fact that the taking of Bagdad would mean a direct blow given to the then continuously successful operations of the Kaiser and his government. It would be a very bold man who would criticize now the strategy and operations of these past days. It is sufficient to say that the attempt was made and was not successful. The Turks were reinforced from Bagdad and the British had to retreat to Kut-el-Amara.

"At Kut-el-Amara, a little mud-walled town of about 5,000 people, lying in a bend of the Tigris, General Townshend, not previously in command of the British forces, was surrounded, and he and his small band of heroes kept the Union Jack flying through the never-to-be-forgotten

days between Dec. 7, 1915, and April 29. Cooped up in this Arab village on rations which gradually dwindled to a few ounces of meal and a little horseflesh per head per day, under conditions of living so terrible as to be almost indescribable, under daily shell fire from the Turks and with constant losses from sickness and disease, these men, by their defense, blocked for many valuable days the German plans in the East.

"It is probable that the effect which this noble defense at Kut had upon the whole war situation, and particularly upon the position of affairs in Turkey and at the Dardanelles, will not be fully understood and appreciated till after the war. Tremendous efforts were made to relieve the beleaguered force, but the absence of all essentials to make the campaign a success, the necessity for the importation of all material by sea from India or Europe, and the lack of all transport facilities in the country prohibited success. After untold privations, General Townshend surrendered, his last communication to his troops reading: 'Whatever has happened, my comrades, you have done your duty; the whole world knows that you have done your duty.'

"What may be called the second campaign in Mesopotamia opened when the late General Sir Stanley Maude, who had taken over the command of the British expeditionary force in August, 1916, began his famous drive to the north in December of the same year. Long and bitter was the fighting at Sheikh Sa'ad and other famous battlefields below Kut. Eventually the Turks were defeated, Kut was retaken, and in March, 1917, after crossing the Diala River, an operation bitterly contested by the enemy, the weary and war-worn troops expelled the Turks from Bagdad and pursued them to the north. Thus, at last, Bagad fell to the allied cause and a definite barrier was forever placed firmly across the German path to Eastern dominion and to worldwide conquest.

"Mesopotamia is the cradle of the human race, a country covered with the ruins of past ages, a land in which eight empires have risen and fallen and in which numerous races, from the Hittite to the Turk, have in succession struggled for supremacy. Here Nebuchadnezzar held his court at Babylon and the writing on the wall was made visible. Here Cyrus the Persian released the captives of the princely tribe of Judah and gave them the opportunity of returning to their native land. Here the Romans under Marc Antony were defeated; here the Greeks under Alexander the Great established an eastern empire, and here Haroun-al-Raschid held his court.

The home of Abraham, of Issac, and of Jacob; the scene of the fiery furnace of Shadrach, Meshach, and Abednego; the country which produced corn and oil for all the world, and which was famous for its beautiful gardens and its wonderful system of irrigation, under the blighting misrule of the Turks has become a country of desert and desolation.'

"But already a change is beginning to creep over the land. The Arab is being taught that justice does not require to be bought, and that it pays him to work.

"The Allies have one great asset to their credit in connection with this war; they have made possible civilization in the desert, and have shown the path of progress to all beholders, holding out to the remnants of the great peoples of the past the hope of a future in their own land under a benign and stable form of government."

Turks Retreat on Tigris – October 26, 1918

British Army in Mesopotamia Resumes Operations.

LONDON, Oct. 25.- An official communication dealing with the operations in Mesopotamia, issued by the War Office tonight, says:

On Oct. 18 we were in contact with Turkish forces holding a strong position astride the Tigris, near Fatah, where the river flows through the Jebel Hamrim country. On Oct. 23 the enemy retired northward under cover of darkness toward Losfrzab (?) pursued by us.

Our forces on the main road to Mosoul by way of Kerkuk drove the Turkish cavalry out from Tauk and advanced to within four miles of Kerkuk.

WASHINGTON, Oct. 25.- The Turkish force occupying Tabriz, Persia, is about to evacuate the city, according to a report dated Oct. 22 from Teheran, which reached the State Department today. The Turks already are withdrawing their forces along roads leading out of Tabriz.

The same report states when the British evacuated Baku some time ago it was almost thirty-six hours before the Turks arrived. In the meantime the Tartars had looted and murdered indiscriminately, and it was reported that thousands of Armenians were massacred.

Asia Minor Divided By Secret Treaties – January 3, 1919

France and England Agreed Upon Zones of Assistance to the Liberated Peoples.

RUSSIA ONCE INCLUDED

She Was to Get Constantinople, but Not Now – Treaties Otherwise Considered Still Alive.

By CHARLES A. SELDEN.

Special Cable to THE NEW YORK TIMES.

PARIS, Jan. 2.- What Foreign Minister Pichon referred to in his recent speech in the Chamber of Deputies as "more recent contracts" between England and France, by which French rights were established in Asia Minor, was a group of secret treaties made by England and France at London in 1916 and another group, made by England, France, and Russia at Petrograd in 1917, just before the Russian Revolution.

According to the London treaties, France has control of all of Syria and Lebanon and part of Armenia, and England in Mesopotamia. Arabia is to be an independent kingdom. Palestine is to have an international administration. All such portions of Asia Minor covered by these treaties as are now part of Turkey are to be taken from Turkey altogether and determination of the exact boundaries of the reduced Turkish area left to the Peace Conference. The peoples of Lebanon, Syria, Armenia, and Mesopotamia are to have forms of government of their own choosing, with France and England acting as advisors in their respective spheres of control.

A French authority on these matters, who explained the gist of the treaties to me, laid emphasis on the fact that the word "control" is to be understood strictly in the French sense, rather than the British.

"That is to say," he continued, "France does not propose to dominate, or have protectorates, or assume rights of colonial Government over Syria and Lebanon, but merely to assist and advise those peoples in the management of their own interior politics. We have a perfect right to do this, for we have helped these countries since the time of the Crusades in the tenth century. We have schools and many interests in them.

"What we propose now is something entirely new in relations between small and great nations. We do not speak of zones of control, or domination, or spheres of influence, but rather of zones of assistance. It is necessary to have some such supervisory assistance, because there are so many different races in these countries that it would be fatal to allow any one of them to dominate the others.

"The treaty of 1917, to which Russia was a party, is now invalid so far as Russia is concerned, because of that country's collapse. The treaty provided that Constantinople was to go to Russia. As it is now, the future status of Constantinople will be fixed by the Peace Conference.

"Other provisions of the Petrograd treaty, pertaining to England and France, still stand. They, too, have to do with our areas of assistance in Asia Minor."

I asked my informant what Pichon meant when he said France recognized the rights of the Peace Conference on this subject of Asia Minor. He replied;

"That means that France recognizes the right of the conference to have a voice in the concrete application of the principles involved in these Asia Minor agreements. The principles themselves and the spirit of these treaties are already in accord with President Wilson's principles. By application of them I mean actual determination of boundaries and zones of assistance in Syria, Lebanon, and the other regions involved."

Secret Treaty Gave England Supervision of Mesopotamia – January 7, 1919

PARIS, Jan. 6.- Supervision of the affairs of Mesopotamia after the conclusion of peace was assigned to Great Britain by a treaty concluded between France and England concerning the future of Asia Minor early in the war. The existence of this treaty only recently has become known publicly, and no previous mention has been made of the important country of Mesopotamia.

Under the terms of this treaty France was to assume direction of the destinies of Syria, Lebanon, and Armenia Minor, (that part of Armenia to the west of the Euphrates.) Palestine was to be under international protection, while Mesopotamia and portions of the Arabian peninsula were to be under the supervision of Great Britain. It was settled that the largest possible autonomy would be assured to the races and peoples in these countries, and an economical administration and equality of rights were also agreed to.

What disposition the Peace Conference will make of this and other secret treaties is much discussed in Paris.

A Plea from Mesopotamia – January 9, 1919

WASHINGTON, Jan. 8.- Representatives of the Assyrian Christians and natives of Mesopotamia in the United States have submitted to the State Department for transmission to the Peace Conference a petition asking that Mesopotamia, including the provinces of Harput and Diarbekir, be placed under control of America, England and France until such time as the people are able to govern themselves independently.

Shelter 50,000 People in Mesopotamia – January 20, 1919

British, by Canal, Also Open 300,000 Acres to Cultivation Near Bagdad.

LONDON, Jan. 19.- Thousands of refugees from Armenia and Eastern Syria were sheltered and fed by the British Army in Mesopotamia during the war, the work being of such a character that it has been made the subject of a special report issued here today. The statement follows:

"The future destiny of Armenian and Eastern Syrian peoples who have taken refuge with the British in Mesopotamia is one of the problems which the Peace Conference must consider. At present in the British refugee camp at Baqubas, thirty-three miles from Bagdad, the British are providing for 45,000 people of both races.

"The work of feeding, clothing, and housing these refugees, when the British were still at grips with the Turks not many miles away, was a triumph of organization. The sudden influx of some 50,000 people into regions already devastated by the ravages of war created a situation of utmost difficulty. The camp at Baqubas was hastily laid out, and in three weeks the refugees were taken in at a rate of 1,000 per day. Sickness was rife and all the refugees were in an emaciated condition.

"Providing clothing and food for these additional members, when so much transport was needed for operations along the Tigris River, was a marvellous achievement. Today the camp is organized as efficiently as many Western towns, the water supply and sanitation is perfect and three hospitals, all modernly equipped to meet medical requirements, are in operation. Nearly 1,000 orphans have been provided for and the whole population of the camp is beginning to recover from the horrors of their exodus from their native lands.

"To return them to the same state of insecurity in which they lived so long would be an international crime against these people.

"An important new irrigation project was opened on Jan. 10 at Mansureyah, on the Dialea River, some seventy miles northeast of Bagdad. Six months ago the British Irrigation Department commenced widening the channel of the river there.

"The new canal is six miles long, and, without further work on it, water can be supplied for the irrigation of 300,000 acres and render cultivation possible as far as the neighborhood of Bagdad.

"The opening ceremony was carried out in the presence of many Arab landowners, who hailed the completion of the work as striking evidence of the good intentions of the British. The increase in wealth to the land thus irrigated will certainly be considerable, and the increased production of food will be of great importance."

Arabs Look to US for Independence – January 22, 1919

Prince Feisal of Hedjaz Says Eyes of the Whole East Are Turned Toward America.

PRESENT CLAIMS AT PARIS

Proposes a State Comprising Hedjaz, Syria, Mesopotamia, Yemen, and Nejd.

PARIS, Jan. 21, (Associated Press,)- Prince Feisal, son of the King of Hedjaz, whom he represents at the Peace Conference, is pressing his claims for the recognition of the Arab State of Hedjaz.

"The Arabs have long enough suffered under foreign domination," he said to The Associated Press today, "The hour has at last struck when we are to come into our own again. We have, I believe, an even greater right to become free and independent than any of the new States to be formed through the war, since we are the oldest democracy in the world.

"The country is inhabited almost exclusively by a homogenous set of Arabs, all descending from a common stock, while the foreign element is infinitesimal, certainly smaller than in any other country I know of. There are only about two thousand Turkish officials and no Turkish population in a land containing three and one-half million Arabs. Why then should not the Arabs rule the country where they live and have lived for countless generations? Why should we not be masters in our own house?"

The Prince then explained that the provinces they claimed as constituting the proposed State are Hedjaz, Syria, Upper and Lower Mesopotamia, Yemen and Nejd. He made it clear that he was here officially only as the representative of the Kingdom of Hedjaz.

"But," he added, "I am also the representative of the whole Arab army, which was recruited from each and all of these States, and I can truthfully say that the Arabs are unanimous in claiming their independence. If the Peace Conference should doubt this statement, or lend ear to the rumors that Syria prefers the French, or Palestine the British, let them send a commission to investigate. If they find that any portion of Arabia would prefer to be ruled by China, Japan, Chile or any other power, then I shall not have another word to say.

"As a small struggling nation we have already done much. King Hussein, my father, commonly called "The Grand Old Man of the East," declared war against Turkey when she was at the height of her military glory, and invited volunteers to his standard. Soon quite a considerable army collected, which, under my personal leadership, inflicted on the Turks a series of defeats, culminating in the taking of Medina last week.

"The Arab Army acted as the British right wing, and in the last offensive, in addition to taking 40,000 prisoners, by a rapid march cut the Turkish line of retreat, enabling the British to capture 70,000 more.

"The two usual objections made to our ambitions," continued the Prince, "are: 'Have your people reached a high enough standard of civilization to govern themselves? and 'Will you have enough money to carry on your State?'

"To the first I unhesitatingly say 'Yes.' The world must not forget that it is largely Arabs that govern the country at this very moment, and all over the world Arabs have shown their worth as merchants and administrators. There must be some six or seven thousand Arabs fighting in the American Army, as there are about 250,000 Arabs in America.

"As for the second question, I also answer in the affirmative. Our country is a rich one. It contains large quantities of copper, iron, mineral oils, and a little coal, while, when properly irrigated, it is perhaps one of the most fertile in the world. That, I think, is enough to tempt capital, and we intend to welcome all foreigners who come with the intention of investing capital or teaching us something. The only stipulation we make is that there shall be no intrigue, no foreign control, but complete freedom for the Arabs.

"I address this appeal to the American people," said Prince Feisal in conclusion, "because I believe American public opinion to be the chief factor in deciding our fate. I also address them because I have complete faith in them. Even in the furthest corner of my own distant country the word has spread that America is the friend of all oppressed and the enemy of all oppressors, that to her all oppressed may come, sure of finding patient ears to listen and strong arms to uphold the weak if the claims are found to be just.

"At this moment the eyes of the whole East are turned toward America. It is up to her now to show that our faith is not misplaced."

For Aid to Assyrians – January 26, 1919

American Bishops Urge Their Claims Be Heard.

Fifty-four Bishops of the Protestant Episcopal Church in this country and fourteen in Canada have cabled to the Archbishops of Canterbury and York a petition to use their influence to obtain recognition by the Peace Conference of an Assyrian delegation to present the claims of the Christians of Mesopotamia, Kurdistan, and Persia for protection and rehabilitation. Professor W. W. Rockwell of the Union Theological Seminary stated that the project had the approval also of the American Committee for Relief in the Near East, and financial assistance to the extent of $1,000 was set aside by Theodore Roosevelt, just before his death, from the Nobel Peace Prize of 1905.

Professor Rockwell also made public a cablegram on behalf of 70,000 Assyrian Christian refugees from Persia begging that the Peace Conference grant their demands for repatriation, protection, indemnity, and the return of prisoners of war. They have designated as delegates to Versailles the Rev. Isaac Yonan of Urumia, with Paul Shimmon of New York as alternate.

Mesopotamia – January 26, 1919

To the Editor of The New York Times:

As a native of Mesopotamia I cannot let the statement in today's TIMES of Prince Feisal of Hijaz pass without being challenged, hoping you will be as generous in giving space to a Christian from Mesopotamia as you have been to a Mohammedan from Arabia.

The inhabitants of Mesopotamia are not Arabs, but descendants of the old Babylonians and Assyrians. Before they were conquered by the Arabs the natives of the Tigris-Euphrates valley spoke Syriac, a sister dialect of the Assyrian language. Like the people of Syria they are referred to as Arabs simply because Arabic is their vernacular. For this reason Arabia has no more right to rule the land between the two rivers than China or Japan.

Mesopotamia is now in England's hands, and the Mesopotamians are only too glad to have their native land remain under its present owner. To England they have always looked for political deliverance, because they know by what they have seen in India that the rule of the English is just. Let, therefore, all Mesopotamia, upper and lower, remain under the control of its present guardian until such time as the natives are able to govern themselves.

ISYA JOSEPH.
Port Chester, Jan. 22, 1919.

90

Near East Refugees in Pitiable Plight – February 2, 1919

Dr. Harry P. Judson Describes Condition of 25,000 Who Marched 700 Miles.

ALL SOCIETY BROKEN DOWN

Soldiers of Dispersed Turkish Armies Have Become Bandits – Anarchy Rules, He Says.

The establishment of a totally new civilization and governmental structure for the Near East to supplant the harsh features of Turkish rule should not be overlooked among the many problems to be considered by the proposed League of Nations, said Dr. Harry Pratt Judson, President of Chicago University, speaking yesterday at the luncheon for the workers in the $30,000,000 drive of the Committee for Relief in the Near East, held at the Bankers' Club. Dr. Judson went to Persia for the committee last Fall, and returned from abroad last Friday.

Dr. Judson said he had made a carefully planned trip through all of Persia and European Turkey, and had found some 25,000 refugees, Syrians and Armenians, along the banks of the river Tigris. The able-bodied men among them were aiding the British in building roads, he said, and those who were left to struggle for themselves were mostly women and children. When they reached the Tigris they had wearily marched 700 miles through storms, wind, and rain.

"They had nothing but scraps on their backs," said Dr. Judson, "and so, worn out, hungry, and exhausted, they reached the camp. The little children had been carried on their mothers' backs, some had died on the way and some could still be seen toddling along the road. There were a thousand pictures one could see of conditions in Turkey, or what, God will, will never be Turkey again.

"We found, for instance, all society broken down, all its foundations worn away, people wandered in the mountains, sleeping under Wintry skies and dying by the thousands. This is the result of centuries of tyranny. We must reconstruct society from the foundations. The problem is not simply shifting a society or Government where there is one already established. It is a case of establishing order where none exists.

"The Turkish armies are broken up and the former Turkish soldiers have become robbers and bandits and anarchy rules with them. There is no peace, no safety, no assurance of life from day to day. That must be taken hold of and made over. And here is one of the great tasks of the allied nations. All the old injustices must be wiped out for all time. We must establish justice and order, and then, of course, we must give them life. None of the conditions in the shaken and disturbed parts of the world draws so upon our heartstrings as does the Near East.

"I believe there can be built up in that land a country worth while, a new civilization on the ruins of the old. They need guidance, help, but first of all, they need life – they must eat, they must be clothed. In this work of generosity and wisdom America must not be left out. We must find out that our duty lies beyond the boundaries of the United States – we found that out when we entered the war. This problem America cannot shake, and she must lend a helping hand."

Charles W. Vickery, Secretary of the committee, announced that Secretary Baker had promised to cable President Wilson for authority to use an army transport to take supplies and relief workers to the Holy Land. Mr. Vickery said Mr. Baker made the promise yesterday in a telephone conversation with Alexander J. Hemphill, Chairman of the Near East Committee.

In the national drive, Mr. Vickery said, Ohio had oversubscribed its quota of $500,000 by nearly $1,500,000. H. W. Jessup, Captain of Team 3, reported that he had received a weekly contribution of $5 a week from a clerk, or half the weekly salary of the donor. A total of $250 was reported from the Greek American Institute pupils, who held a campaign last week. About $14,000 was received in small donations at the headquarters of the committee, 1 Madison Avenue, yesterday.

News from Mesopotamia – February 9, 1919

To the Editor of The New York Times:

We have often heard of the urgent need of Armenia and Syria, and now that the Near East drive is on again we are reminded of the intense distress of the Armenians and Syrians, but almost nothing is said of the Mesopotamians. Yet their situation is not one bit less intolerable.

The first letter since the outbreak of the war has just arrived in America from the city of Mosul, across the Tigris from Nineveh, which was occupied by the British Army shortly after the armistice with Turkey was signed. It is interesting to note that the letter went by air service to Bagdad, some 200 miles south. It opens with "Glad tidings to you, because the British are here," and tells of the great joy that has filled the hearts of the inhabitants, particularly the Assyrian Christians, by the elimination of the Turks from the fair Province of Mosul. Prior to the entrance of the British the situation of the Assyrian Christians had reached the critical point. Some noted Christians, among them D. Saaty, who for many years was a resident of Providence, R. I., and from whose letter to his relatives in Providence I gathered my information, were about to be hanged, when suddenly British cavalry seized Mosul.

On the terrible conditions described in the letter it is enough to say that one-fourth of the population has perished from starvation and epidemic. After speaking appreciatively of the wonderful changes wrought by the new Government within a short time, Mr. Saaty closes his letter with a humble supplication that the British may stay in his native land, and stay forever.

The Assyrian Christians and natives of Mesopotamia all over the world, in recognition of the humanitarian work of Great Britain, have selected England to serve as an administrator over their native country and have decided to petition the Peace Conference to place under English control also the second Province of Diarbekir, in Upper Mesopotamia.

ISYA JOSEPH.
Port Chester, N. Y., Feb. 9, 1919.

Curzon Defends Policy to Russia – February 21, 1919

Condemns Parley with Moscow Over the Heads of Archangel Government.

BRITISH TROOPS NOW SAFE

Great Work of Relief in Asia Minor Described to the House of Lords.

LONDON, Feb. 20.- In the course of the debate in the House of Lords today on the Near East and Russia, Lord Curzon said that the Tschaikovsky Government would regard it as incredible treachery if the Allies negotiated with the Central Government at Moscow. He described the Bolshevist soldiers as "ruffianly bands, murdering and massacring wherever they went," and declared that it was impracticable to negotiate with them locally.

There was plenty of food in Russia, said Lord Curzon, but the Bolsheviki utilized their control of arms and food to terrorize and desolate.

In closing the debate the Marquis of Lansdowne expressed grave misgivings over the prolongation of operations, and said that an honorable termination would be generally welcomed.

Replying to the comment of the Marquis of Lansdowne on the position in North Russia, Lord Curzon strongly condemned the suggestion that the British Government should open negotiations with the Bolsheviki over the head of the Archangel Government, while, he contended, there was good reason for the Prinkipo proposal, whether it succeeded or not.

The proposal to deal with Russia piecemeal would have calamitous results, he said. The Bolsheviki were trying to dispose of the provincial Governments one by one, and wanted to release the forces in the north so that they could send them against General Demikine, head of the Government of Ekaterinodar.

Lord Peel, representing the War Office, described the military situation in North Russia. He said that the recent retirement on the Archangel front had been carried out with very little loss, either of men or material, while the enemy had suffered heavily. There was no immediate anxiety regarding the safety of the forces there. Technical troops were needed for the distribution of food and other supplies, and steps were being taken to furnish them. If the Bolsheviki continued their aggression it might be necessary to reinforce the allied troops.

Lord Peel said that there had been comparatively little sickness and few cases of frostbite among the allied troops, who had had the advantage of Sir Ernest Shackleton's experience of training men for arctic life.

Viscount Bryce asked the Government for information regarding the present condition of the Asiatic provinces of the Ottoman Empire, and what measures had been taken by the allied Governments for the protection of the unarmed Christian population of those provinces.

Lord Curzon, in reply, said that he would endeavour to relieve any anxieties regarding the areas over which the political influence of the Allies extended, namely, Mesopotamia, Syria, and Palestine.

"In Mesopotamia," he said, "we have now been securely established for over two years. The advance made in that time in the development of that country in respect of irrigation, agriculture, the introduction of agricultural machinery, the education of children, in fact, in the development of the country from every point of view, has been amazing. More has been done in two years than was done in the five preceding centuries, and it is a proud experience to those Englishmen who go to Mesopotamia to do their share in this great work.

"Similar work is being done in Palestine and Syria. The same progress is being made, roads have been made or remade, railways have been laid, wells have been dug or reopened. The country is paving its way and is enjoying prosperity which it never had and never could have enjoyed under Turkish rule."

With regard to the outlying regions of the Turkish Empire, Armenia, Cilicia, Anatolia, and Asia Minor generally, he could only say that he would not like to prejudge the ultimate decisions of the Peace Conference. In Armenia great hardships were being endured by the inhabitants, which were intensified by the scarcity of provisions and by lack of means of communication. Missions had been sent out and were doing excellent work, but ardent as were the sympathies of the Allies with these people, if they embarked upon an arduous, lengthy and costly campaign in Asia Minor he ventured to think that there would be a good deal of protest.

At present there were in Syria and Palestine more than forty thousand unhappy refugees. In Mesopotamia there were forty thousand Armenians and Nestorians, in Mosul seven thousand, and in Trans-Caucasia more than 45,000. Altogether there were 150,000 refugees being kept from starvation by this country.

The policy of the Government, said Lord Curzon, was to repatriate the refugees, but that could not be done until communications were very much improved. An American mission had come with ships laden with food, clothing, medicines, and agricultural implements and was making its way into the East through ports from which these regions could be reached.

There was no reason to be dissatisfied with the part England was playing in that work, Lord Curzon said, and he thought that the British officers, soldiers, sailors, and, in fact, all concerned, were not merely carrying out necessary duties, but were engaged in a work of charity and mercy.

British Relief in the Near East – February 23, 1919

Huge Sums Expended by That Government in Aiding the Destitute.

ARMY FUNDS DRAWN UPON

Gen. Marshall's Headquarters Alone Fed 45,000 – Responsibility for Russo-Armenians Disclaimed.

When the British armies advanced their lines into enemy territory in Syria, Mesopotamia and other countries in the Near East so many thousands of refugees who had been despoiled by the Germans and Turks came under British care that the facilities of the private charitable agencies were unable to relieve all the suffering. It was necessary for the British supply service to aid. A partial story of its relief work has now been revealed in the request for more funds for the stricken populations, and in the announcement that all the work of the British army and the British charitable associations will be continued in co-operations with American relief organizations.

In Mesopotamia, General Marshall has made himself responsible for the feeding and welfare of about 45,000 Armenians and Jews from the headquarters at Bajubah. All the money has been provided by British army funds. Included in the sum spent there is a grant of 220,000 rupees ($75,000) for blankets and necessities for women and children who were starving when they came within the British lines. A similar number was cared for by the British armies in Palestine and Syria with money taken from the army funds and with gifts from individuals.

General Sir Edmund Allenby estimated that $125,000 a month would be needed for relief work south of Aleppo. General Thomson undertook the work in Baku, where he began the repatriation of refugees under great difficulties.

Charitable associations in this country and Europe have pointed out in their pleas for funds to carry on the work in the Near East that the problem of caring for these stricken populations was thrust upon the allied countries when the races were relieved of Turkish oppression and brought within the British lines. When the refugees in thousands came under the British flag the problem of Armenian relief was created.

The greater number of refugees thrown upon the care of the British Army were in Mesopotamia and Syria. In Mesopotamia the majority were Assyrian fugitives, and those in Syria were Armenians who had

been treated brutally by the Turks. Others, less welcome, were the Russian Armenians and the Assyrians of Urumia.

Great Britain, partly by reason of her vast pre-occupations in the East and Far East, has from time immemorial been expected to take a leading hand in the "relief" of Eastern peoples devastated and desolated by the horrors of war. This has been particularly true since the Russo-Turkish struggle of 1877-8. But there comes a time when even the greatest of great powers must call a halt, and the Government of Great Britain has found it necessary to state categorically that it can assume no responsibility either for the fugitive Russian Armenians or for the Assyrians in the Urumia area who incurred Russian animosity while Russia yet remained an organized power.

It will be remembered in this connection that directly after the collapse of Russia as a factor in the world war the British Government sent out a military mission to the Caucasus with the object of rendering organized help to such of the population as were prepared to band together in a real resistance against the Turks under the (then) Trans-Caucasian Government. That attempt failed, the failure being directly due to the inability of the Armenian, Georgian, and Tartar peoples to form any kind of a co-operative league or coalition. At the same time it enabled the first British expedition to Baku (August, 1918,) to be carried into effect.

A terribly long line of communications, the inability to provide sufficient troops after the Russian debacle, and the wretched fighting quality of the Armenian and other auxiliaries caused that expedition to be withdrawn from Baku. But the conclusion of the armistice in November helped materially, inasmuch as its Clauses 11 and 15 enabled Great Britain to fill the place left vacant by Russia, and thus to insure the protection of the Armenians by the expulsion of the Ottoman power. Incidentally, the British advance into Persia also enabled them to save the lives of the greater number of the Assyrians of Urumia.

On of the chief difficulties in aiding the populations is the lack of transport, but the relief agencies are now taking up that problem and it is expected that sufficient money will be provided from British private and official sources and from American private charities to relieve all suffering. The British military authorities already have notified the American Mission for Relief in Asiatic Turkey and other relief organizations in this country that they may expect the fullest co-operation in their relief work in the Near East. They will be invited to co-operate with all the British agencies and it is believed by workers in those countries that, with the money to be made available for the use of the British army, sufficient funds will be available to cover all relief in the territories taken by General Allenby and General Marshall.

War's End Brings No Relief From Outrage To Armenians and Syrians in Persia – March 30, 1919

The American Committee for Relief in the Near East announced yesterday that advices from Persia received within the week indicated that there had been no cessation of the persecution of Christians by fanatical Moslems. The committee has received a message from the Azerbaijan Relief Committee at Teheran, forwarded by the American Legation at Teheran, through the State Department, to the national headquarters of the Near East relief organization here, which says:

"Three hundred Armenian and 200 Syrian women at Khoi have been forced to accept Mohammedanism. One hundred and seventy-one absolutely destitute Christians in most abject misery are at Salmas. One thousand Christians, remnant of Uramia, furnished relief without personal supervision. A great many Christian women and girls are captives in Persian Kurdistan. Over 300 villages in the Uramia-Salmas district are deserted, and a great many have been demolished by the Mohammedans, who are continuing devastation.

"Over 25,000 receive daily relief allowance at Tabriz, and thousands more are imploring help. Relief of Christian remnants, repatriation of scattered refugees, return of captives, and reopening of Uramia as a relief centre must depend upon assurance of safety, life, and property, which Persia seems unable to give. Rehabilitation needs enormous sums, but any expenditures for this purpose under the circumstances would be most probably lost because of constant disorders and impotent Government."

In a statement the American committee explains that the districts mentioned are the Armenian districts in North-western Persia. The attitude and behaviour of the Persian Kurds is not considered surprising by those in close touch with the relief work here.

"Dr. Stanley White, Secretary of the Presbyterian Board of Foreign Missions," the statement adds, "declared before his departure to Asia Minor that this same element had tried unsuccessfully to bring Persia into war on the side of the Central Powers. This was prevented, in Dr. White's opinion, only by the efforts of the American missionaries and relief workers in that country."

The committee announced the following contributions: Mr. and Mrs. Edwin Thorne, $2,000; Mrs. William L. Moore, $1,000; Mrs. Jeremiah Thorne, $900; W. V.

S. Thorne, $500; Schweir Relief Committee, $500; Riverdale Country School, $500; Anonymous, $500.

Persia's Debit and Credit – June 29, 1919

Present Claims on the Allies and Her Aid to the Enemy

New York, June 24, 1919.
To the Editor of The New York Times:

It is now eight months since the armistice was signed. Peace, thank God, has at last been restored between the Allies, America, and Germany, but in the remote regions of so-called neutral Persia we are informed by an American entitled to know that at present it is not safe for any native Christian to go to Urumia and Salmas, where all villages are absolutely deserted, both by Moslem and Christian, and the former Garden of Eden is ruled by brigands of the type of Villa.

Urumia and Salmas are the back door of Persia to Kurdistan. It is a most beautiful and fertile region in the northwestern part of Persia bordering on Turkish Kurdistan, some 200 miles or less southeast of Mount Ararat, and about 150 miles northeast of Mosul and not very far from the lake and city of Van, the ancient capital of Armenia. For four years the region has been trampled under foot of Russian, Turkish, Kurdish, Assyrian, and Armenian soldiers. The British have at last found a place there and in other parts of Persia.

During all these years Persia has claimed that she was neutral. Her Central Government has nominally been so. But German propaganda has so blinded the average Persian that he makes believe he is neutral, while Persians of Tartar and Kurdish origin have been fighting side by side with the Turks and Germans, against Russians, Englishmen and their auxiliaries, the Assyrian and Armenian peoples. Some of the blackest acts of this war were perpetrated in this region, acts that compare with and surpass some of the brutalities in Turkey and elsewhere. These acts were committed by Persians encouraged by the Government in the province of Azerbaijan. Indeed, the Persians stopped only when they knew it for a fact that the war had been won by the Allies and that there might be a reckoning for the acts committed against those who were fighting on the Allies' side. Among such acts may be mentioned the murder of Mar Shimun, the Assyrian Patriarch, by Simku, the Persian Kurd; the murder of Archbishop Sontag, the Apostolic Delegate of the Pope to Persia, and with him 600 persons, by Arshad-i-Humayoun, an officer of Persian gendarmerie. The former took place in Salmas, and the latter at Urumia in Sontag's own home and mission.

It would probably be unfair to blame Persians for all that has taken place at this remote region of Persia, where the Turks and Kurds were strong. But there must be drawn a line between the Persians of whom we read in the classic books of Iran and these Tartar or Ajam (Turkish) Persians in northwestern Persia. After four years of bitter struggle in these regions the fact remains that these Persians are equally responsible for the destruction of property and the taking of life. The Central Government was on the verge of declaring war on the Entente long before the collapse of Russia. The revolution in the latter country emboldened the Persians, and when the Russian frontier crumbled it was difficult to restrain Persians from their admiration and profound sympathy for everything German.

The relation between the Persians and their fellow-countrymen, the Assyrian (Nestorian, Chaldean) and Armenian Christians, was formerly a pleasant one. But it was that of a peasant to his landlord, where the Christian had very little say in the matter of common interest to both. He was tolerated and allowed to live and exist as a profitable tenant. This is no place to relate the work of the various missions and what they did for the whole community, Christians and Moslems alike.

But the coming of the Russians put a different complexion on the whole situation. As their influence grew stronger, the feeling of the Moslems toward the Christians changed, especially when there was any talk of the rights of the Christians. After the declaration of war the sympathy of the Christians remained with the Allies, while the Persians, on the whole, sided with the Germans and Turks. On the withdrawal of the Russians in 1915 the Persians plundered and killed Christians, in some cases rivalling Kurds and Turks. As the Christians had never undertaken any hostile acts against Persia, the latter, as a neutral, should have seen the situation and not suffered it, dealing fairly with them. But this was too much for them, and soon they drifted into the arms of the Turks and became their bitter partisans.

The things came to a crisis in the Spring of 1918, when the German onslaught in the West was at its height. Its effect on these remote regions was like magic. The Persians could no longer be restrained. The Russian Revolution having caused the crumbling of the Caucasus battle lines, the British, French, and a few Russian officers, urged the Assyrians, who had come from across the border after they were driven out by the Turks, to take up arms and stop the rush of the Turks through Persia toward Baku and the Caucasus. To this the Assyrians and the Armenians of the region responded loyally, believing it to be their duty to stand by the Allies at their dark moments. In all their battles the Christians were more than victorious. In this the Persians not only sympathized with the advancing Turks and Kurds, but actually began hostilities and encouraged and helped the Turks as an ally. In twelve battles the Assyrians were more than victorious and maintained their own. At last the Armenians of Van had to retire, and after Salmas was also left to the enemy they combined to protect Urumia till their ammunition became exhausted, and they had at last to withdraw south with some 75,000 men, women, and children. The Persian nobles and officers joined in the pursuit of the refugees, and many Christian women are even now in Moslem harems. The Persians share the responsibility of these cruel acts with the Turks and Kurds.

The object in writing this letter is not to cast blame on the Persians, blames worthy as they are, but to call the attention of America and others to a peculiar problem arising in a corner of Persia in the dealing with which Persia is utterly incompetent.

Persia is claiming additional territory to its extensive possessions. It wishes to extend to Turkestan, to the Caucasus, and to Kurdistan, but she is not able to keep her own house in order. She rightly asks for 33,000,000 francs indemnity for State property lost during the war, and 3,509,000 for private property. But what of the Christian population, who have lost all? And most of what they have lost was found in Persian homes. The Kaiser and his leaders are to be brought to the bar of justice, but what of the murderous Persian Kurds and Tartars, whose crimes are, we are sorry to say, only too plain?

The Persians have been busy maligning the Christians, who have no representative at the Persian court, to such an extent that they have till now prevented Christians from returning to their homes. Surely the Allies have a duty to these people. Are they going to listen to Persian tales and expatriate the Christians who have left their vineyards and their possessions, and are dying to return?

Are the Persians really neutral? Have they been pro-ally? Have the Allies no other duties than to allow Armenian and Syrian committees to feed these people on their crumbs. Will they get any indemnity? Why should they lose 70 per cent. of their effectives?

There are a dozen men at Paris pleading the cause of these people. Let us hope the daydawn of freedom and security is not far off.

PAUL SHIMMON.

No Massacres by Persians – August 10, 1919

To the Editor of The New York Times:

In your issue of June 29, 1919, a letter is published bearing the signature of Paul Shimmon, containing unwarranted attacks upon the Persian Government for what is alleged to be Persia's responsibility for Urumiah troubles. The charges made are so obviously false and the misrepresentations made in the article so glaring that they contradict themselves even to the most superficial reader, and the Department of State at Washington has on file formal notices from the Assyrian associations in America disclaiming Paul Shimmon as their spokesman.

The article charges the Government with having "encouraged" the Persians in the Province of Azerbaidjan to take steps against the Assyrians of Salmas and Urumiah. This is absolutely false. The Assyrians of Urumiah will themselves testify to the spirit of toleration and benevolence always shown them by the Government as long as the Government of Azerbaidjan was free to act. But the public should remember that for a number of years previous to the world war, and in the teeth of repeated protests of the Persian Government, the armies of the Czar unjustly occupied most of the districts of Azerbaidjan and supported and held in office notorious reactionaries whose misdeeds were calculated to justify the Russian occupation. This not only paralyzed, but practically annihilated, the authority of the Persian Government in those parts. Then, when the war broke out, and, at the request of the Allies, Persia declared her neutrality and insisted upon the evacuation of her territory by Russian troops, her just demand was utterly rejected and ignored by Russia. This furnished Turkey the excuse to follow suit and invade Persia with her armed forces to fight the Russians. This state of things provoked a general confusion which not only eliminated every remaining vestige of Persian authority in Azerbaidjan, but subjected the country to the dire consequences of famine, massacre, and ruin entailed by the violation of Persian neutrality by the neighboring belligerents.

Among the acts of foreign aggression was the arming of the Christian population in the northwest and the attacks made upon the Moslem inhabitants – formerly in perfect peace with their Christian neighbors – for which foreign intrigue had paved the way. Persia lodged energetic protests against all these acts of aggression with all the allied powers, but no step was taken by the powers to effect the withdrawal of foreign troops from Persian territory and respect that country's neutrality and thus enable the Persian Government to check the terrible conflagration which cost the lives of a vast section of the population and the loss of hundreds of millions in property.

Now to attach any responsibility to the Persian Government for wrongs done in the occupied zones would be too ridiculous even to deserve notice were it not too cruel to be ignored.

The wrongs suffered by Persia are recognized even by Russia, which was at the time the greatest author of Persia's ruin. In fact, at the outset of the war, when Persia protested against the Russian occupation of the country and disclaimed responsibility for all ensuing wrongs, Russia officially shouldered the responsibility and promised to indemnify all those suffering losses from her invasion of Persia. This places the unfounded charges made by a so-called sympathizer of Persian Assyrians in their true light.

As to the death of Mar Shimoon, the facts filed with the Foreign Offices of the allied Governments prove that Mar Shimoon was killed while making an attack upon the town of Salmas, on which occasion many thousands of unarmed Moslems lost their lives. He would have been spared had he not put himself at the head of an armed force on the neutral soil of Persia.

As regards the troubles in Urumiah, again there is a tendency to forget that the hardships endured by Christians and Moslems alike were due to the abnormal conditions created by the world conflagration, which spread into Persia against her will, and by reason of the violation of her neutrality; moreover, much of the harm done was brought about by the Christians themselves. Djelou tribesmen, who are Christians, followed the Russian troops out of Turkey into Persia, were armed by the Russians and, in spite of the Persian Government's protests, remained on in the Urumiah district after the Russian retreat, with an increased equipment of cannon and ammunition. These wild and unbridled tribes abandoned themselves to all kinds of cruelty and depredation toward the Moslems, whom they massacred by thousands; the town of Urumiah was destroyed by them and much property was looted. The murder of Mgr. Sontag was much deplored by the Persian Government, but it is absolutely unfair to throw the onus of responsibility for this dastardly act on them and quite untrue to say that any officer of the Persian Gendarmerie was implicated in the assassination of the Apostolic Delegate.

As regards the "additional territory" Persia is alleged to have claimed before the Peace Conference: To begin with, the chief claims of Persia consist in the indemnification of her people for the damages suffered from the belligerents who converted the country into a theatre of war. She further claims guarantees for her judicial, economic, and political independence, which has suffered from unjust foreign attacks for over a century. The so-called "additional territory" constitutes but a part of the patrimony of Persia which has been, on various occasions, wrested from her by foreign aggressors.

The claims for indemnity referred to in the article are true except in the amount, which is far below the estimate which has hitherto been made of the enormous losses sustained by the country and people. Persia courts a commission to be appointed by the Peace Conference to go to Persia, to inquire into the charges made concerning the Urumiah matters, and invites an estimate to be made of the devastation wrought by the war, which made the country the Belgium of Asia. It will then be found that the indemnity asked is not only a minimum of losses suffered, but it is essential for the reparation of regions where hundreds of thousands are homeless and reduced to dire indigence.

MIRZA ALI-KULI KHAN, LL. D.

Charge d'Affaires of Persia at Washington. With the Persian Peace Mission at Paris.

Paris, July 26, 1919.

Assyria and Persia: A Reply – August 17, 1919

By the Rev. PAUL SHIMMON.

To the Editor of The New York Times:

Your readers are greatly indebted to you for an article entitled "No Massacre by the Persians," which appeared in your issue of Aug. 10 signed by Mirza Ali Kuli Khan, Persian Charge d'Affaires, defending the cause of the Persian Government against what I wrote in your issue of June 29.

It is well to hear the Persian version and their point of view of their treatment of the Christians and their supposed neutrality. But let me throw some light to your readers on certain facts that are historical and that are testified to by neutrals and which will stand the test of time.

Azarbaijan is the northwestern province of Persia bordering on Russian Caucasus and Asiatic Turkey. That it was battle ground for the Russians and the Turks, and its Government was thoroughly pro-German, and consequently their hatred of the Christians whose sympathies were with the Allies was made evident during the course of four years. The situation became critical on Washington's birthday, 1918. At that time there were no Turks and no Kurds prowling upon the plains of Urumiah and Salmas. The struggle was between the Persians and their passion for everything German and Turkish and between the Christians with their sympathies for the Allies. The Governor of Urumiah, Ijial-ul-Mulk, seriously and solemnly advised the Assyrian National Committee that if they would come to him he would take them to Mosul to Marshal Mackensen and ask pardon for what the Assyrians had done and that they should not be further deceived by the empty promises of the British. Later on, the Persians proposed that the Assyrians should give up their weapons or leave their country.

In vain did the Assyrians plead for time and mercy when the opportunity would permit of their leaving the country. An attack was attempted on the home of Agha Petros, Commander in Chief of the Assyrian forces, by the Persians, who were well prepared and who attacked all quarters of the city. Agha Petros pretended defeat until the Persians were within reach of his machine gun, operated, it is said, by his own mother. Within twenty-four hours the Persians found themselves utterly hopeless. Headed by their Governor and city officials, white flag in their hands, they passed the American Mission grounds and were escorted to the home of Mar Shimun and sued for peace.

Arrangements were made, everything was satisfactory. Mar Shimun left for his home in Salmas. The whole of Salmas plain, including the Governor, came out to escort Mar Shimun to Diliman as if they were escorting a king.

In the meanwhile, the Government of Azarbaijan sent Visouk-al-Mamalik and Salar-al-Mamalik, the latter the Chief of the Persian Cossacks, as a delegation of peace to meet Mar Shimun in Salmas, and they had a private message for him from the Government of Azarbaijan. Their only condition, it was reported, would be that the Christians should be disarmed and that they would be allowed to remain in the country in peace. When the delegates met the Patriarch, Mar Shimun, they were so much impressed by his chivalrous spirit, by his splendid carriage, and kingly ways, that they were captivated by his charms and never said a word about disarming his people, and they parted to meet again.

In the afternoon another meeting with Ismael Agha, (commonly known as Simku,) who is the head of a powerful tribe of Shekak, was arranged, when the Patriarch with some seventy men went to Kuhna Shahr, (ancient city,) a little town on the outskirts of Diliman, to make peace arrangements with the Kurds. When Mar Shimun left he and his men were shot from the tops of the roofs by the servants of Simku. Only a few of them escaped, among them David, a brother of Mar Shimun. The Patriarch was killed and mutilated beyond recognition. When the Christians in other localities saw horses running pell-mell, saddled but without any one riding them, they then knew what had taken place. Later on, when the Christians had taken the Castle of Chara, where Simku had his headquarters for years, they found his correspondence sufficient evidence to show how far the Azarbaijan Government was implicated in this matter.

It is from now on that the famous battles of the Assyrians in Salmas and Urumiah took place. The whole world stands astonished at their magnificent fighting qualities. They never turned their backs to their enemies, and the admiration of the Persians was so great for them that they called the Assyrian army "Kuchuck Alliman," (meaning little Germany,) showing how highly they thought of Germany as a fighting nation. Up to the present the struggle was only between the Persians and the Assyrians, and the initiative was always taken by the Persians and the Assyrians were always on the defensive. During the succeeding thirteen battles, lasting to July 31, 1918, the Persians, the Kurds, and the Turks combined together against the Assyrians, who were cut off from the British and the Russians and knew nothing of what was going on outside of their own immediate locality. One does not wish to mention the name of those neutrals who were on the ground and who knew the whole facts, and who have always reported them rather quietly, of which reports we wish to take no advantage to reveal their names, for their testimony is invincible and corroborates literally all that I have written above.

The assassination of Mgr. Sontag is even more revolting. Frenchmen and Roman Catholics the world over should tolerate no condoning of the foul murder of the apostolic delegate, a man known for his piety and non-interference in political matters, a living saint and martyr.

Mgr. Sontag had, during the times of disturbances, sheltered Arshad-i-Humayun, a Persian gendarme officer, and his men, and kept them for months in the magnificent French Mission quarters. Before the arrival of the Turks, about 11 o'clock, Arshad-i-Humayun, according to the story of one who was among the inmates of the Mission, shot Mgr. Sontag twice. He then took hold of the money belonging to the Mission in the safe deposit vault. Bishop Thomas Audo was shot once and died after three days. Bishop Mar Petros, with some priests, escaped and on the arrival of the Turks was held in prison.

According to the testimony of the neutrals again, some six hundred persons were killed. They were mostly killed with clubs, spears, and axes, and this before the arrival of the Turks and Kurds. Later on, when the Turks arrived, they found Bishop Mar Petros and three of his priests still remaining alive, they kept them in prison, and when they found out that these men could testify to what they had actually seen of the murder of Mgr. Sontag, and who it was done by, they allowed them their freedom.

Of about some 10,000 Christians who were stranded and remained in Urumiah and Salmas in July, 1918, all perished except about 1,000 of them, sheltered by an Assyrian woman worthy to be called a Joan of Arc. To be sure, there have been always some good Persians whose memory we shall cherish forever.

There is not a single Christian in Urumiah and Salmas today, where their homes had been long before the dawn of Mohammedanism. If there is any grain of justice left in the breast of Americans, Frenchmen, and Englishmen, if there is any compensation for acts of chivalry, if there is any reward for loyalty of a nation, then the Assyrians deserve the first place of honor for what they have done for civilization on the Persian-Turkish frontier. They have lost their head, who was their King and their

Archbishop. They have lost their homes. They have parted with all the earthly goods they had and over 60 per cent. of their numbers. What other nation has given so much?

PAUL SHIMMON.
Representative of the Assyrian Patriarch.
New York, Aug. 13, 1919.

Death of Mar Shimoon – October 1, 1919

To the Editor of The New York Times:

My attention has been called to a letter in your issue of Aug. 10, bearing the signature of Mirza Ali-Kuli Khan. Your correspondent refers to the murder of Mar Shimoon, the Syrian Patriarch, and says that "the facts filed with the Foreign Offices of the allied Governments prove that Mar Shimoon was killed while making an attack upon the town of Salmas." The facts filed with the allied Governments prove nothing of the kind.

I have before me a copy of a telegram, dated March 26, 1918, sent by the British Consul at Tabriz to a prominent personage in London, which reads as follows: "Mar Shimoon, the Syrian Patriarch, from Turkey, was proceeding to Salmas when he was met by Simku, who invited him into his house and there shot him dead."

I have resided some considerable time in Persia, and my experience is that the Persian Government, when called upon to account for some crime perpetrated in their country, have often forwarded "facts" to European Governments which were a pure romance. I have no doubt whatever that the "filed facts" as to the death of Mar Shimoon are one of these romances. Before the Shah is allowed to set foot in either America or Great Britain he ought to be brought to book for encouraging Simku, one of his subjects, to murder Mar Shimoon.

Mirza Ali-Kuli Khan has gone out of his way to attack Mr. Paul Shimmon, and says that "the Department of State at Washington has on file formal notices from the Assyrian associations in America disclaiming Paul Shimmon as their spokesman." I do not know the secrets of the Washington State Department, but I wish to say that I had before me in 1915 the original document appointing Mr. Paul Shimmon the representative of the Assyrian people in America. This document was in Syriac and bore the seal of the late Mar Shimoon and I translated it into English.

F. N. HEAZELL.
Chuch House, Westminster, London, Sept. 8. 1919.

Would Send Here 30,000 Homeless Nestorians; Britain Has Been Caring for Persian Refugees – March 8, 1921

Special Cable to THE NEW YORK TIMES.

LONDON, March 7.- The British Government is asking the United States to agree to the emigration of 30,000 Nestorian Christians to America. They are descendants of the ancient Assyrians and as a result of the chaos created by the great war have left their homes near Lake Urumeyas in Northwest Persia and have been living in camp under British protection in Mesopotamia.

Local conditions make it impossible for them to return home and the British Government has notified the American Near East Relief Committee that it cannot undertake to continue the aid it has given them after April 1, but would be willing to pay half the cost of transporting the Nestorians to America.

At a conference held at the Colonial Office today Dr. James Barton, representative of the Near East Committee, pointed out serious difficulties in the way of the British plan. It would be necessary to have special legislation passed by Congress to get the immigration laws relaxed for this purpose.

Plight of the Assyrians – June 19, 1921

To the Editor of The New York Times:

Before the war the Assyrian race numbered about two hundred thousand. Encouraged and incited by the British, they fought against their neighbors, the Kurds and the Persians, in support of the allied cause. They have thereby incurred the undying enmity of those two races. Their sacrificial contribution to the allied cause is mutely evidenced by the fact that about thirty thousand of these people grouped around Mosul and Bagdad, far from their homes, are practically the only survivors. Forty thousand Armenians now at Basra are in similar condition for the same reasons.

Last year they attempted to return to their homes, but they were turned back by the Kurds. The Arabs will not permit them to remain where they are. British protection is being withdrawn. England and the United States have refused admittance to them. There is no other place for them to go. Unable to stay where they are, and unable to move, their chances are almost equal to those of the proverbial snowball on the kitchen stove.

We are not anti-British, any more than we are un-American, in protesting against particular phases of our own Government's policy, but perhaps our humane sentiments can be aroused to the point of action by the plight of these human beings.

EDWARD TYLER PERRY.
Westfield, N. J., June 16, 1921.

Seize Reputed Priests in Chaldean Frauds – July 26, 1921

Paris Police Arrest Two Men Said to Have Collected Big Fund for Alleged Relief

PARIS, July 25. – In the arrest tonight of two men, alleged to be Chaldean priests, the police say they have uncovered fraudulent collections in France and the United States amounting to many millions of francs.

The men, according to the police, confessed that on different occasions they had called on the Rev. Frederick W. Beekman, rector of the American Church in Paris, to collect funds for Chaldeans persecuted by the Turks, each with a letter supposed to have been signed by the Archbishop of Palestine.

Before their operations in France, they are said to have confessed, the men had been in the United States, where they obtained many thousands of dollars from the Episcopal clergy and a large number of prominent laymen.

1,000 Assyrians Coming in Small Sailing Ships – August 6, 1921

Some of the Survivors of 75,000 Who Fled From Persia Now on Their Way Here.

WASHINGTON, Aug. 5.- More than a thousand Assyrian Christians, fleeing from persecutions by Mohammedans, are on their way to the United States, on small sailing vessels, Secretary Davis said today. According to information reaching the Department of Labor, he added, they are part of a party of 75,000 who started to march from the interior of Persia to ports, 25,000 of whom died on the way.

Those who survived boarded available vessels that were leaving for Japan and the countries of Europe and America. The thousands coming here, the Secretary said, will be far in excess of the quota for Persia, against which country they should be charged under the percentage Immigration law, but he added that no decision had been reached as to what would be done with them.

Swindle American Rector. – November 21, 1921

Two Men Posing as Chaldean Priests Convicted in Paris.

PARIS, Nov. 20. – Two men posing as Chaldean priests, Sleevo Brekha and John Pacha, have been condemned to eight months' imprisonment on the charge of swindling the Rev. Frederick W. Beekman, rector of the American Church in Paris.

The men were arrested last July while collecting funds supposedly for Chaldeans persecuted by the Turks. Their arrest, according to the police, disclosed fraudulent collections of this kind in France and the United States to the amount of many millions of francs.

Hold 'Rev.' Danoo as Relief Grafter – March 5, 1922

Immigrant With Many Aliases Accused of Collecting $4,000 as Near East Aid.

Posed as Nestorian Priest

Ministers and Prominent Men Victims – Forged Names of Donors on Credentials.

The "Rev." John H. Danoo, arrested several days ago in Mooretown, N. J., was arraigned yesterday in the Third Precinct Court in Newark before Judge D'Aloia, charged with obtaining money under false pretenses. He was held in $2,000 bail for the Grand Jury.

Danoo was arrested on the complaint of Julian Zelchenko, State Secretary of the Near East Relief, who alleges that the prisoner has been victimizing ministers and prominent men throughout the country by representing himself as an agent for the collection of funds for the Near East Relief. The police say he has collected at least $4,000 in this manner.

Samuel Barbaria, an Inspector of Immigration at Ellis Island, told the police that the prisoner arrived in this country in 1917 from Syria under the name of John Isaacs and went to Hartford, Conn., where he worked on a farm. Later, Barbaria said the immigration authorities learned that Isaacs was collecting money for the Near East Relief without authorization. He was brought to Ellis Island for deportation, but released on his promise of good behavior. Barbaria said the next he heard of Isaacs was that he had escaped from an insane asylum in Hartford. The Inspector said he would arrange to have Isaacs deported.

The police found among Danoo's effects letters of recommendation, a list of contributors and notes from ministers commending his work. According to the police, after receiving a donation the prisoner would get the contributor's autograph in a book and forge signatures to letters of recommendation written by himself.

The specific complaint against Danoo is that he obtained $12 from the Rev. John C. Donnell, pastor of St. Thomas's Episcopal Church, Newark. Dr. Donnell said Danoo appeared in church as the Rev. George A. Jordan, a Nestorian priest. Danoo donned vestments and was about to preach when he apparently recognized some one in the congregation, discarded his vestments and left.

The police say that Danoo, who is known under many aliases, says he is a deacon in the Nestorian Church. Among the contributors listed in a book found in Danoo's possession are the following: Austin G. Colgate, Bishop William T. Manning, George Gordon Battle and Robert L. Pierpont.

New America Club Wants "More Liberal Quota" for Armenians and Assyrians – April 23, 1922

Boston, Mass., April 17, 1922.
To the Editor of The New York Times:

In THE TIMES of April 15, under the caption of "Armenians Not Massacred," the Armenian High Commissioner at Constantinople is quoted on the authority of the Secretary of Labor and the Secretary of State as stating that after four months' careful investigation he is unable to find any proof that seventeen women and children deported from the United States in excess quota last September were outraged and massacred in Turkey.

The massacres of those women and children and many other massacres of a similar nature have taken place in Turkey. In fact, the history of the past fifty years of Armenian Christian life in Turkey has been one succession of outrages and massacres by the Moslems. It is well known that a Mohammedan acquires merit in his religion in the ratio of the number of Christians he has outraged and murdered.

Although several months have elapsed since the statement made before the House Immigration Committee by C. V.

Knightley of Boston, the High Commissioner's denial that such massacre took place was not made public until the day the consideration of the quota law came before the Senate.

Unfortunately, due to a printer's error on Page 193 of the report of the Immigration Committee where the word "trip" was used, instead of "ship," the report reads as though these women and children were deported to Constantinople on board the S. S. Gul Djemal of the Ottoman-American Steamship Company. This, however, would not be possible, as the Gul Djemal made but one trip to the United States after the quota law came into effect. She carried back to Constantinople twenty-eight deported aliens in excess of quota. As the statement before the committee shows, the Ottoman-American Steamship Company ordered these passengers returned to Ellis Island, and the Gul Djemal brought them back. They were afterward admitted under temporary bonds, and are still with their families in the United States.

The letter presented to the Committee on Immigration and printed in its report is sufficient evidence that one family was wiped out in the massacre. This letter was dated from Constantinople and at the time it was presented, Mr. Knightley did not know where the aliens had landed further than this, that the Commissioner at Ellis Island stated they had been deported to Constantinople. However, it was afterward shown to the committee in a letter to the chairman, that these seventeen aliens had landed further than this, by a Greek Steamship Company, and afterward transferred in a local boat to Marsine, Turkey. These people belong to Aintab and Marash. Marsine was their nearest port. They were landed without money and must walk and provide themselves with food on their journey to Aintab; the first town at which they could hope to get assistance was Adana. It was on their way to this town that the massacre took place.

We must concede that it would be a difficult matter for the American High Commissioner to obtain evidence of any particular massacre, seeing that these outrages are taking place all the time. There is no excuse, however, for the American High Commissioner's report that they had interviewed the persons who were deported on the Gul Djemal and that they found them alive and well. As previously stated, the aliens deported on the Gul Djemal were returned to this country and she has not made another trip from that day to this, so the foundation of the report is entirely wiped out.

There are five families in this country whose relatives were massacred at this particular time. If the Secretary of State or the Secretary of Labor requires proof that they were massacred, their relatives in the United States can supply the same, and one would think that they would have been consulted.

It seems to us that the United States Commissioner at Constantinople is there to serve the interests of business and commerce, and he can best do this by playing Turkish politics and supporting Turkish propaganda. We can supply evidence to the State Department that Admiral Bristol, the American High Commissioner at Constantinople has, at the request of Turkish officials, compelled American commercial steamships that have taken on board Armenian Christians, who had been driven to Turkish ports by the onslaught of the Turks, to deliver them on shore again and leave them to their fate. We can also show that several American missionaries have been massacred by the Turks while carrying out their mission of mercy to the Armenians and Assyrians. It is not the policy of the State Department to embroil the United States in disputes with foreign countries by taking up questions as to the sacrifice of human life in any foreign country.

Proof was obtained from relief workers that this massacre of Armenians took place, and several other massacres, two of them quite recent. We were asked, however, by the Near East Relief and the Armenian Relief and other welfare societies not to make public these reports, as it would bring down upon them the wrath of the Turkish officials and make it impossible for them to continue administering relief to the starving and suffering people of Armenia. This reason was given by relief workers who testified before the Immigration Committee for omitting the names of those who supplied information.

In justification of our efforts to secure a more liberal quota for the Assyrian people who have fought so bravely to uphold the Christian religion in Turkey and Persia and were awarded only 78 quota for any one year, we wish to say one word. These people, of whom there are about 15,000 in the United States of America, make excellent residents of our country. They are peaceful, industrious, saving and have no desire to crowd in our cities. Some six or seven hundred of their wives, children and near relatives are awaiting an opportunity to join them in this country. Their passports were visaed before the quota law came into force, and for months they have been kept in various seaports at the expense of their American relatives.

To show that this works an injustice to the United States of America, we would mention one family in Chicago. There are seven members in the family; the youngest is attending school, the other six earn $107 a week. Of this amount they must send to Marseilles, France, $50 a week to maintain in idleness three sisters who, if permitted to enter this country, would be able to earn their own living without competing with any American. The $200 a month would be placed in our savings banks or used in the purchase of food and clothing, thus increasing the demand for labor in the City of Chicago. This case is mentioned to show how this shutting out of dependants is a drain upon the economic resources of America.

The Treasury Department reports that last year, $145,000,000 was deposited in Government savings banks conducted by the Post Office Department. Of this amount, $36,000,000 was deposited by American-born native stock; the balance, $109,000,000, was deposited by our alien population. All the labor performed on our street cleaning and repairs and 90 per cent. of the menial labor in the country is performed by aliens. The children of these aliens are being educated in our schools. They will be citizens of the United States some day. They will not take the place of their parents in the performance of menial labor.

We are not in favor of throwing open our gates to a flood of immigrants. We think, however, that consideration should be given in any renewal of the quota law to those of our own flesh and blood whom we must support in idleness in foreign countries unless we have a more liberal administration of the quota law. We would rather support these people in the United States of America and we could do this at one-fourth of the cost.

The New America Club represents citizens of the United States from twenty-seven different European countries.

THE NEW AMERICA CLUB,
By ANTHONY J. EMERY, President.

Assyrian Immigration – June 4, 1922

New York, May 1, 1922.

To the Editor of The New York Times:

In THE TIMES of April 23 appeared an article on immigration matters, signed by Anthony J. Emery, for the New America Club of Boston, representing twenty-seven different European countries. I wish to thank Mr. Emery for his contribution, at least in so far as it deals with the Assyrian people, of whom the world has heard but little in comparison with the Armenians, but whose gallantry in war and suffering for their race is superior to that of any other allied nation.

Some people have even doubted the existence of such a people and have often mixed them with their fellow suffering brethren, the Armenians. But the Assyrian people are distinct as French are from English and, in fact, more so.

The Armenians are supposed to be of European extraction. The Assyrians, on the other hand, are descendants of the old Assyrian Babylonean and Chaldean people, from whose home civilization started in the Valleys of Tigris and Euphrates. The language of the Assyrians, even from the times of Daniel the Prophet, has been the Aramaic or the Syriac, which to the present day is the language of their liturgies and Prayer Books. For that reason, sometimes they are mixed up and called "Syrians," even though they live hundreds of miles east of what has been known as Syria in history. Very few Syrians in Syria speak Syriac, while most of them speak Arabic, but for that reason they would not be called Arabs, no more than Americans would be called English because they speak the English language.

In the matter of the immigration there has been an unintentional injustice to the Assyrians which has hardly been realized by the American lawmakers. The Americans make law for their own protection. As an American of over twenty-five years' citizenship I have always taken a very deep interest in immigration problems. I believe that we have done right in face of European collapse to limit immigration to America. But here is a situation in the case of Assyrians (and Armenians as well) hardly paralleled in history. These people have shed their blood and have suffered the most sublime martyrdom of any age. This has been due in ninety cases out of one hundred to their sympathy and stand for the allied cause.

The fortunes of war have been so in the Near East that

European nations for various reasons and at various times were compelled by the exigencies of the times to side now with Persians, now with Turks and now with Arabs and Kurds. The Assyrians and Armenians, on the other hand, have been compelled to fight all these Moslem races, not only for religious principles, but also as a matter of self-preservation and for political and racial reasons. It may be easy for the French to make terms with the Kemalists as against the Greek and British, it may be easy for the British to take the mandate of Mesopotamia and look after the Arabs now as they did a few years ago yearn to make a lasting friendship with Persia. But the suffering people of God have always been the Armenians and the Assyrians. Had the Allies left them alone they might have gotten on with the Moslems in some way or other. But that has not been the case. These people have been loyal and their loyalty has been bought dearly.

America has had a benevolent influence in the homeland of these people, in Armenia proper, Turkey, Persia, &c. They knew of America through the missionaries and thought of America as a country of wonderful opportunities. So, in spite of the unwillingness of missionaries, they have began to come to America, and, as testified by those who can judge they have made the best of citizens.

A tragic situation took place about the Assyrians of Persia and Mesopotamia. During the uprising of the Arabs against the French and British, it was found necessary to pacify these men of the desert. So the British and the French were compelled to act friendly toward these. The Assyrians themselves long and pray for peace and desire to return to their own former homes.

The British did make an effort to send them back to Persia. But it was late in the season, and when their leader, with his army, was advanced well nigh toward Urumia, in Northwestern Persia, they were compelled to return for lack of food and from cold, for fear of meeting the fate of Napoleon in Moscow.

Long before this took place, in the Fall of 1920, the people from Urumia were driven out from their homes in 1918. Some five to ten thousand of them were left in Urumia together with American missionaries. Of these, in the course of the next ten months, only 630 were saved, and that only through the bravery of Gordon Paddock, the American Consul at Tabriz. Mr. Paddock is now in America and can well testify to these facts that I am now telling. He can tell as to whether there have been massacres in those regions or not.

Through their wanderings when the Assyrians and Armenians of these regions despaired of any hope of returning to their homes and when the American Congress refused the mandate over Armenia, there was nothing left for those who had part of their families here but to come to America. The American Consul at Bagdad visaed their passports up to July 3 last. They started on their trips quite innocently and while in India, Japan, France and Constantinople the law of three per cent. was passed debarring these people from joining their families. The Assyrian quota as per the present law is only 78 persons. An effort is being made to allow each nationality a minimum quota of one thousand persons. In this way all those stranded in the various parts of Europe and Asia will be allowed to join their near relatives, and this will relieve some of the cruel separation entailed in the present law and admit some elements of mercy in the just cause of immigration.

It is quite natural for us in America to find fault with the European nations dealing with the Near East. But it must be confessed that America has great moral responsibilities in that country. By refusing to take mandate over Armenia we retarded the progress of a gallant people for one hundred years. America missed the most wonderful opportunity of developing a nation in the cradle of civilization and in the home of Christianity. England took Palestine, Arabia and Mesopotamia under her mandate. France is doing her best in Syria. Armenia was offered to us to nurture and to develop. To the one hundred million Americans this was a proposition of which they knew next to nothing and naturally they did not venture. The Senate Committee on Foreign Relations – and so the American Congress – refused the mandate. Two things are left to us now. First, to feed the orphans, which America is doing in a most wonderful manner under the auspices of the Near East Relief. This work shall go to the credit of the United States as the most monumental of its kind for the Near East. The future of those lands will be changed by the little children America has saved from the roads and highways and has lodged them in schools, hospitals and industrial centres.

Second, the present immigration regulations work very great hardship on those whose families are partly here and partly abroad or on the roads. If the minimum of 1,000 for each nationality is also passed by the House of Representatives, as I understand has been passed by the Senate, then we will have mixed the quality of mercy with our stern sentence on immigration, and these people who are stranded on the roads will join their relatives and thereby save American money from being spent in Europe and elsewhere.

PAUL SHIMMON.

Turks Bar Hearing of Armenian Plea – December 27, 1922

Allies Give Unofficial Audience to Noradunghian, Kemalists Being Absent.

THREAT TO SUMMON IRISH

Riza Nur Bey Makes It in Ridicule of Armenians' Lack of Standing in the Conference.

LAUSANNE, Dec. 26. (Associated Press). – Armenia was the storm centre of the Near East conference today. The Turks refused to attend a meeting of the sub-commission which had arranged to hear the plea of the Armenians for the establishment of a national home in Turkey, and both Ismet Pasha and Riza Nur Bey sent strongly worded communications to the conference protesting against the decision to allow the Armenians to state their case.

They declared that if the Armenians, who had no official standing and represented no independent Government, were heard by the conference, there was no reason why the Egyptians or the Irish should not be allowed to present their demands.

The so-called irregular Egyptian delegation has been waiting in Lausanne for more than a month for permission to be heard by the conference and voice a demand for the independence of Egypt and complete withdrawal of the British army.

Text of the Turkish Protest.

The Ottoman protest, signed by Riza Nur Bey, was addressed to President Montagna of the sub-commission on minorities. It reads:

"In the official program for today which was received by our delegation I read, not without surprise, that the Armenian and Bulgarian delegations will be heard by the sub-commission on minorities. At the end of the last meeting of this sub-commission I presented objections to your plan to hear the Bulgarian delegation, and it was agreed that the Bulgarians would be received privately by the Allies. Now I learn that you not only intend to receive the Bulgarians at the sessions of the sub-commission, but also to hear the Armenians. I protest energetically against these audiences.

"If, despite the unchangeable attitude of the Turkish delegation, which has a direct interest in the proposed discussions, your Excellency insists upon listening to these two delegations, I cannot agree that this meeting should be regarded as official, or that the declarations made should find a place in the official report of the conference.

"From the official standpoint and the standpoint of the Turkish delegation the session must be considered non-existent. The conference exists of two parties. The Allies constitute one party and Turkey the other. Therefore any session at which Turkey is not represented cannot be regarded as official.

"Despite the logical arguments which I furnished the other day in support of our position, you have decided now to hear the Armenians as well as the Bulgarians. The Armenian delegation is composed of Turkish subjects, and it pretends to represent Armenians who are Turkish subjects. To enter into contact with such a delegation would be equivalent to employing against a State subjects of this same State. Any initiative or a step in this direction will only encourage us to support the assurances which have been showered upon us in connection with the safeguarding of our sovereign rights. Furthermore, it would be helpful to inquire what can possibly be the official character of the Armenians who have been invited, and of what Government they pretend to be the delegates.

"The existing State of Armenia has already arranged with Turkey, by treaty, all differences existing between them. As Lord Curzon himself has declared, the Armenians now petitioning the conference are private persons who are opposed to the Armenian Republic of Erivan as they are to Turkey.

"The sub commission on minorities is going outside the field of its rightful deliberations. The Turkish delegation believes itself justified in not participating in these meetings.

"If the principle is accepted that all private persons who pretend to be delegated by their respective countries are to be heard by the conference, then the delegation of the Government of the Grand National Assembly of Turkey will have the honor to propose, by the same token, the admission and audience of delegations representing the populations of Egypt, Palestine, Syria, Irak, India, Tunis and Tripoli and the Moslem minorities of Jugoslavia, Rumania, Bulgaria and Greece, as well as the delegates of Ireland, who ceaselessly ask our assistance to secure an opportunity to present their just and legitimate claims."

Heard at Unofficial Session.

In consequence of the Turkish protest the official meeting of the sub-commission was postponed, and the representatives of the inviting powers, Great Britain, France and Italy, sitting alone, listened to the Armenian spokesman, who suggested that a home be established in the northeastern vilayets of Turkey, which should include historic Mount Ararat, or a section in Cilicia. It was impossible, he declared, for the proposed Armenian home to amalgamate with the Armenian Republic of Erivan, which had been taken over by the Russian Soviets. The Armenians would willingly accept the same relationship with Turkey as the dominions with England. In conclusion he asked for exemption from military service for the Armenians and urged the maintenance of the Orthodox Patriarchate in Constantinople.

The Entente delegates took the Armenian petition under advisement, as they did petitions from the Bulgarians and the ancient people known as the Assyro-Chaldeans.

Noradunghian Pasha, once Turkish Foreign Minister, presented the Armenian plea. He said that the tragic events of 1915 had widened the gulf between the Turks and the Armenians. The young Turk Government at that time had not only used unspeakable methods in dealing with those Armenians who were loyal subjects of the Ottoman Empire, he asserted, but it also lacked the most elementary understanding of the interests of the country. Although Armenians were serving in the Turkish army, there were many deportations of Armenians and suppression of a great part of the Armenian population without the slightest pretext.

"We deeply regret that mutual distrust still exists between the Turks and the Armenians," he continued, "and that nothing is being done by Turkey to diminish the gravity of the situation. It is impossible for us to consider as a solution that the refugee Armenians who are in foreign countries should return to Turkey, as Ismet suggests."

"There is, on the one hand, the fate of the Armenians of Balikesri, Brusa and Bigha, who, on assurances given them by their Turkish countrymen, decided to remain in these localities and lost their lives as a result of recent events. There is, on the other hand, the present exodus of the few survivors of the 1915 deportations, who, after the signature of the Mudros armistice, had the courage to return to Anatolia.

"Those unhappy people are once more obligated to leave the country. We cannot imagine that in midwinter these women and children and old men, without means of sustenance, are fleeing of their own free will to the Black Sea ports or to Syria, while the able-bodied men are being kept in concentration camps or at work."

700,000 Armenian Refugees.

"There are now about 700,000 Armenian refugees in the outlying countries. Of these 345,000 are in different parts of the Caucasus, 95,000 in Syria, 120,000 in Greece, the Aegean Islands and Macedonia; 40,000 in Bulgaria and Western Thrace and 50,000 in Persia, the remainder being dispersed here and there, not to mention about 110,000 orphans, who providentially are receiving aid from the American Near East Relief.

"All these refugees have lost many relatives by violence. Every one awaits with anxiety and legitimate impatience a solution which will end the tragic situation. Those refugees, once laborious productive elements, are now cared for by benevolent institutions, and it is quite clear that this pitiful situation should not last indefinitely.

"These are the unhappy facts: You will see that they are not of a nature to re-establish confidence or make possible the return of these families to the country where they formerly lived and where they will only find poignant memories, bitterness and inextricable dissensions. No kind of permission or order, no kind of proclamation or special stipulation can reassure them. Only the creation of a national home would be able to obliterate the tragic past, allay accumulated hatred and bring back confidence.

"It is these considerations, and also a desire to keep their formal pledges, that have led the allied Government's in the conferences in London in March, 1921, and Paris in March, 1922, to decide to constitute an Armenian home. We cannot imagine that the Turks, who have struggled for independence and have recognized the independence of the Moslem peoples which before the war formed part of their empire, can refuse to other countrymen the right to realize such moderate claims.

"It should be noted that the Turkish State and Turkish individuals have benefited by the real and personal properties of the Armenians who disappeared without leaving successors. We believe that the national pact of Angora, which antedated the project of the creation of this moderate home and did not foresee the present case, does not prevent the Turks from considering impartially and favorably the question at issue and from reaching a solution by the adoption of the same arrangements that have proved successful in a number of countries, particularly the British dominions.

"As for as the territory suggested as a national home, our delegations refer you to the memorandum which they have the honor to present to the conference, in which they have left to the conference the choice between a region in the northeastern vilayets or a region in Cilicia. Both of these are regions with which the Armenians have been historically connected for centuries, and in which the present Moslem populations, owing to the war, are very much reduced.

Allies' Pledges Recalled to Them.

"Let us, gentlemen, remind you that all the peoples of the world have admitted the justice of our cause and have expressed themselves in their Parliaments and through the Assemblies and Councils of the League of Nations as to the necessity of creating a national home. You have there on your tables pathetic appeals signed by millions of members of European and American Christian churches, communities and well-known individuals in behalf of that solution, and it is a particular pleasure to think that there are not only Christians with that thought in mind, but thousands of Moslems in India, Persia and Azerbaijan, and also in Turkey, who on many occasions have recognized the legitimacy and need of an Armenian national home.

"Finally, having examined the question under Turco-Armenian and humanitarian aspects, allow us to mention also in a few words the point of view of righteousness. The allied powers, who made war for the triumph of justice, have on many occasions promised liberation to the Armenians in Turkey. It was after the agreement concluded in London and after the terrible deportation of 1915 that the Armenians of America and other countries were invited to form a "Legion of the Orient" under the auspices of France.

"Having signed enlistment forms, in which the liberation of their country was stipulated, they fought bravely and successfully under the command of Field Marshal Allenby on the Palestine and Syrian fronts. The Sevres treaty, the arbitration of the United States defining the Armenian boundaries and the twenty-second article of the Pact of Nations are so many reiterations, which have consecrated the engagements contracted by the Allies during the war on behalf of the Armenian people.

"If, as a consequence of political events, you are now preparing a new treaty for the pacification of the Near East, we are certain that the spirit which is urging you to take into consideration in a larger way the Turkish claims will also inspire you to recognize the legitimacy of the Armenian cause. We do not doubt that nothing will be neglected in your deliberations and resolutions for safeguarding the principles and promises referred to.

"In conclusion, let us express the wish that the Turkish delegation, newly inspired and more fully enlightened, will modify their views on the question of an Armenian national home which is now before us. To have Dominion will not only be a title of glory for the new Turkey, but she will also have accomplished a just and fruitful act in conformity with all the interests involved. She would gain the friendship of the Armenian element, productively active, which will, in addition, be devoted to proving itself a helpful factor in the future.

"We are thoroughly convinced that it is only by such a solution that the peace concluded for the Near East will have a sound and rational basis and will be prevented from becoming illusory and incomplete."

Plea for 160,000 Bulgarians.

Appearing at the unofficial meeting of the sub-commission, the Bulgarians requested that 160,000 Bulgarians who had fled from Eastern Thrace should be permitted to return to that country, which had become Turkish territory, and said they were ready to accept the same treatment as Turkish citizens.

Biblical history came before the meeting when the representatives of the Assyro-Chaldeans arose. Their people live in Mesopotamia, between Mosul and the Turkish frontier. They wish to maintain their own language and customs and to be allowed to dwell in peace. General Achpitros, their chief spokesman, said with dignity that history had proved that Adam and Eva were born in their country and the early chapters of early life moved about the Assyro-Chaldeans.

The sub-commission also discussed the question of fixing the nationality of the peoples inhabiting provinces detached from turkey, such as Syria, Irak and Palestine. It was decided that Greek and Turkish subjects could have the option of declaring themselves subjects of their own nation within a period not yet determined. After the expiration of this period they would become by reason of their continued residence citizens of the countries in which they resided.

Hopeful progress was made today on the problem of the Greek Patriarchate. The French suggested as a possible solution that permission be granted the Patriarch to remain in Constantinople as an autonomous archbishop, with the understanding that he would in no way represent political or administrative matters, or voice the ambitions or incarnate aspirations of Greece. He would exist as a religious figure only.

The French argued that the brusque removal of the Christian leader would cause an unpleasant feeling abroad toward the new Turkish State. The Turks will give their views on this suggestion at another session.

The Straits problem still remains unsettled. The Allies are striving to arrange some formula for a general collective guarantee that Turkey will not be subjected to foreign aggression. The Turks decline to grant the Straits Control Commission jurisdiction over the zones of demilitarization, as requested by the Allies. There is a general expectation, however, that the Straits problem will be solved, although Russia's ultimate attitude remains a mystery.

LONDON, Dec, 26.- An Exchange Telegraph dispatch from Athens gives Premier Gonatas as authority for the statement that the Greek Government has no thought of acceding to the Turkish demand for the withdrawal of the Greek Patriarch from Constantinople, even if the allied powers accept the Turks' views as expressed at the Lausanne conference.

The Premier asserted that his Government considered the question a national one on which no Greek Ministry could give way.

www.ingramcontent.com/pod-product-compliance
Lightning Source LLC
Chambersburg PA
CBHW062046090426
42740CB00016B/3039